W9-CQJ-028

LIVE INSIDE OUT·NOT UPSIDE DOWN

A DYNAMIC NEW METHOD OF SELF-THERAPY

Consciously Connect to your inner strength and wisdom

FRAN LOTERY PHD & SHERRY MELCHIORRE PHD

Copyright ©1996 by Fran Lotery and Sherry Melchiorre

All Rights Reserved

 Bronze Publishing
1187 Coast Village Road
Suite 1-422
Santa Barbara, California 93108-2794

No part of this book may be reproduced by any mechanical, photographic or electronic process, or in the form of a phonographic recording, nor may it be stored in a retrieval system, transmitted, or otherwise be copied for public or private use—other than for "fair use"—without written permission of the publisher.

Note on confidentiality: All casework material in this book has been carefully disguised to protect confidentiality. All names of patients and subjects are fictitious. No person may be identified from material presented herein.

Publisher's Cataloging in Publication
Lotery, Fran.
  Live inside out, not upside down : a dynamic new method of self-therapy : consciously connect to your inner strength and wisdom / Fran Lotery & Sherry Melchiorre.
    p. cm.
  Includes bibliographic references and index.
  ISBN 0-9647103-5-8

    1. Self-actualization (Psychology) 2. Self-realization. I. Melchiorre, Sherry. II. Title.

BF637.S4L67 1996   158
                    QBI95-20289

10   9   8   7   6   5   4   3   2   1

Cover Design: Therese d'Avignon
Illustration: Diane Greenseid
Book Production: Cirrus Design

Printed and Manufactured in the USA

CONTENTS

BLESSING

DR. ROBERT MULLER
FORMER ASSISTANT SECRETARY-GENERAL
OF THE UNITED NATIONS

May Fran Lotery and Sherry Melchiorre be blessed for having resuscitated, re-enlivened and illuminated a fundamental law of the art of living: that evolution and nature have placed in each human being a dream, a basic task, to fulfill to which we must return when society or the fashions of the day divert us from them. Such a return will yield us untold happiness and fulfillment—which are the rewards of evolution and of the universe for having done the right thing expected from us.

Thus the pleasures and ecstasies of love are given to youth to fulfill evolution's will for reproduction. Thus the love and happiness of a mother are her rewards for life-giving and rearing. Thus the gratifications of love between elderly couples are the rewards for the good they are doing together. Then the leaders of nations, religions, corporations and educators and all institutions will see bloom a happiness nurtured by their dreams and lives devoted to them.

They have rediscovered the fundamental law of nature and the art of living.

We have forgotten that happiness is the reward of the universe and of God for our fulfillment which comes from the inside, from the core of our being. May this rediscovery by Fran and Sherry be blessed with the widest spread and networking around the world, blessing in turn and bringing happiness to innumerable individuals, couples, families, social groups up to the entire human family and its dreams for a peaceful, better world.

If we respect this law, we will enter a millennium of peace, harmony and untold happiness on our beautiful, miraculous planet. Then God and the invisible forces of the universe will be happy with us, for we will have fulfilled the next step of our evolution. This book has a contribution to make—with all my heart I bless it indeed.

[signature]

DR. ROBERT MULLER
CHANCELLOR OF THE UNIVERSITY FOR PEACE IN COSTA RICA
FORMER ASSISTANT SECRETARY-GENERAL OF
THE UNITED NATIONS
June 27, 1995

PREFACE

IT was 1986. The cold war was going strong and cities across the nation were becoming more violent, including our beloved Los Angeles. Although we deeply believed in the spiritual concept of love, acceptance and oneness, we were feeling victimized, judgmental, helpless and fearful. How to translate the spiritual side of us into daily living was the conundrum.

We discovered the answer as well as the challenge in a movement whose purpose was to educate as many people as possible on how to live "oneness." For almost a year, we thought intensely about the concept of interconnectedness and what it means—that feeling whole is not just about handling your own needs. We noticed all the different ways in which we did not experience oneness with other people —how we blamed others for our problems, how we felt competitive or threatened in a hundred everyday situations, and how this did not make us happy. We knew there had to be a way of meeting our own needs and being satisfied, while remaining loving towards others. In the course of countless conversations together, we discussed each and every conflict in our lives and how we could apply the principle, "I will not pose an enemy." As we became more and more entrenched in this new way of thinking, we realized we could no longer view problems in isolation from the whole of humanity, or avoid recognizing how our every action affected others and our environment.

With this awareness, addressing specific problems with clients without addressing their connection to themselves and the rest of the world struck us as analogous to a physician removing symptoms without considering the substance of a patient's life—diet, exercise, work, relationships, emotional states and support systems. .

Our practices shifted into a radical new context, and the seeds for this book were sown. Over time, we developed a process for seeing situations from a clear perspective without anger, fear and resentment. We called this process Conscious Connection^SM. It allowed us to tune into the peaceful, loving, whole and connected place inside, that had always been there—and this felt truly magical.

This proved to be critical in our ability to write *Live Inside Out* ■ *Not Upside Down*. In spite of our individual differences in personality, work style, schedules, and ages, we were able to write together in a way we have since learned is very unusual (we are still best friends). We sat at the computer, talked and wrote as if we were doing an often practiced dance routine, like a couple who had lived together for years, and could finish each other's sentences.

This book is the result of our desire to communicate to others that they too can live in a chaotic, imperfect world with love, acceptance and serenity.

ACKNOWLEDGEMENTS

W E'D like to thank our husbands, Michael Melchiorre and Rex Lotery, for their collaboration, unending patience and practical, thoughtful suggestions. And to our children, daughter and son-in-laws and grandchildren, who have given us so much love and inspiration, we hope that this book will give you hope and confidence for your future. To Joseph Spivack who was a living example of **Conscious Connection**. Each and everyone of you, friends and family, who have contributed in your own special way, know that you are a vital part of this book. We thank you all from the bottom of our hearts. Mary Chesterfield, Jean Stine and Sarah Allaback, we are grateful for your masterful editing.

We appreciate the openness and willingness of all of you who have worked with us both in psychotherapy and workshops over the last decade. We could not have developed this process without you. In order to insure privacy, all the vignettes and examples that we have included in this book have been altered or are composites. All names and identifying information have been changed, therefore, any resemblance between our examples and a particular person is coincidental.

INTRODUCTION

THIS BOOK is based on knowledge and experience we have gained from our clients during workshops and therapy sessions. After many years of counseling, we began to recognize certain characteristics our clients shared, regardless of economic or ethnic background. Difficulties with relationships, work, thoughts, feelings or behaviors were not problems but symptoms, evidence of alienation from the authentic self. Our clients were separated from their true natures by negative thoughts and emotions that had often been established years earlier. This mental/emotional stuff, which we call *counter-connection*[SM], prevents a natural link to the authentic self. When we are not living from the inside out, *counter-connected* thoughts and feelings take control. The external, artificial self seems "normal." Trapped in this upside-down state, we suffer from negative thoughts and feelings, destructive relationships, addictions and other problems.

The solution is Conscious Connection.[SM] Our progress with clients demonstrates that Conscious Connection actually alters mental habits by allowing the authentic, healthy self to take charge. Feelings of insecurity, anxiousness and inadequacy diminish in the face of the powerful authentic self. In the chapters that follow, we will show you how to confront the layers of protection you have built to shelter yourself from pain. With our help, you will learn to break down these external barriers by making a conscious effort to connect with your authentic self. You will learn to live inside out, not upside down.

The success of Conscious Connection depends, in part, on your determination to read and practice the exercises included in this book. As a reader, you are participating in a dialogue that resembles a workshop or therapy session. Throughout this book, we will present examples of clients, your classmates in the learning process, who are successfully dealing with their problems through Conscious Connection. The following case-study illustrates that even seemingly confident, "together" individuals are often battling destructive feelings.

When Dennis M., a forty-year-old computer programmer, strode into the workshop wearing cowboy boots and a jaunty red bandanna, one participant assumed he was looking for the acting school next door. Dennis' easy smile made the other participants feel comfortable; they created a space for him in the group almost instantly. When Dennis spoke about his feelings, the other participants were amazed.

I feel disconnected from others most of the time. It's as if I live in a plastic bubble isolating me from friends and relatives. I don't think anyone would notice if I just faded away. Dennis' voice began to crack. He pulled at the silver clasp around the bandanna and looked around distractedly.

When did you first feel disconnected and alone? asked Sherry.

That's hard ... I've never felt close to anyone in my life, even though there's nothing I want more....

Can you recall the first time you felt this way?

Dennis stared at the floor, one hand in a pocket jingling change. *Once, when I was around ten, my father stormed out of the house yelling. He was hooked on drugs, see, and didn't spend much time at home. When I was there, he either knocked me around or pretended that I didn't exist. That day Dad said he was leaving for good so he would never have to see me again.*

How did you feel?

Totally insignificant ... and alone. I felt like a speck of dirt, a bug about to be squashed. ... Then I pulled myself together. I put on my superhero cape and said to myself, 'I can get along fine without you. Who needs you anyway. I'm more powerful than a locomotive.'

Sometimes, Sherry responded, *when we are over-whelmed by our feelings, we protect ourselves by shutting down and not allowing any feelings. The problem is, that while we protect ourselves from pain,*

*we also keep out joy, love, fulfillment, and other good
feelings. Does that make sense?*

*Sure, but what does my little kid experience have
to do with my life now? That was ages ago . . . I
mean, I never think about it. I just remembered it for
the first time.*

*O.K. Let's go back to the way you said you usually
feel.*

Alone. Insignificant. Just hollow and empty inside.

*And how often do you feel joyful, fulfilled, close to
someone. . . .*

Not too often.

*So even though you have people in your life right
now who care about you, you feel like that little boy
whose father walked out on him. You don't believe
that anyone really cares, no matter what they say.*

Yeah. How can I change that?

The solution we offered Dennis, a way to get back in
touch with the part of him that has the capacity to heal, is
the subject of this book.

During the course of our work with Dennis and other
clients, we made a profound discovery. No matter how
deeply or how long someone had been cut off from the true
self, as soon as he or she began to move toward it, the self
moved also and met the individual halfway.

We also observed that no matter how damaged an individual appeared, even in cases of severe addiction, the
authentic self remained intact. The authentic self has a
strong, natural drive toward health and wholeness. When

sufficiently supported, this true self was strong and healthy enough to set the person's life on the right course and to help him or her stay there. Once clients were reunited with their authentic selves, they became participants in their own cure. Connected clients almost always instantly knew what they needed in order to become healthier, more fully alive human beings. The result was a significant increase in their rate of progress.

Once we identified the problem, we began to explore techniques of contacting the authentic self. Ultimately, we synthesized a number of common elements into the simple, powerful exercise we used with Dennis—Conscious Connection. When consistently practiced, Conscious Connection results in immediate self-empowerment, growth and healing.

You may be wondering what sets this book apart from other methods of "self-help" therapy. The psychological books you find in libraries and bookstores misdiagnose the problem. These books try to convince us that our difficulties are caused by victimization; we are either victims of our environment, our genetic make-up, or some combination of both. Spiritual books, although understanding the disconnection with the authentic self, give us no concrete tools.

As you will see in the exercises that follow, we have integrated psychological and spiritual traditions to create a dynamic new method of self-therapy. It is a study of the soul as well as of the personality. The Conscious Connection exercise is not only intellectual and physical, but also spiritual and holistic. Although the results produce effects resembling those of meditation and deep relaxation, the process goes beyond these techniques to release your innate inner strength, confidence and self-knowledge. When we unite people with the experience of oneness and love through the Conscious Connection Exercise, we teach them how to trust inner knowledge, to clarify values and to transform negative beliefs. The psychological obstacles to maintaining a connection with the soul are removed forever.

Individuals are struggling with the same "symptoms" that plague society. As a world, we suffer from fear, despair, indifference and an overwhelming lack of love and care for our fellow human beings. Like the pain of individuals, the violence, war, abuse, neglect, starvation and destruction on this planet have been misidentified as the problem. In fact, our tragic social predicament is the symptom of a world disconnected from its center. The only way to create a world in which people care for one another is to regain our power as individuals. When you are in touch with your authentic self, you will experience the calm, unshakable part of your being that places you in harmony with others. The key lies in connecting to your essence through the process of Conscious Connection.

Growth

You cannot teach a man anything. You can only help him discover it within himself.

GALILEO

One

DISCOVERING THE SELF

WE have been socialized to believe that inner pain, dissatisfaction and anxiety are part of the human condition. From an early age, we are taught to apply the motto "no pain, no gain" to our mental, as well as our physical goals. We learn to "hang-tough" and struggle, to do anything but "wimp out." While these attitudes may result in success on the playing field, they can leave us feeling emotionally empty, frustrated and dissatisfied. The belief that pain is a necessary component of our lives causes us to develop negative value systems. We measure job success by power and status, not by personal fulfillment. Close relationships with others are sacrificed for career advancement. Sometimes our inner fears become so overwhelming that

we are unable to feel joyful, to celebrate, or even to participate in community life. Along with our daily concerns, we
carry heavy burdens of pain, dissatisfaction and anxiety—
feelings that drain us of energy and hope. Everyone has
experienced all-consuming, relentless battles with negative
inner feelings.

How can we learn to ease this torment and allow ourselves to become happy, satisfied human beings? Popular
self-help books and recovery systems, although they try, do
not offer lasting solutions to our emotional problems. Now
and then a group, book or article speaks about our particular pain and gives us hope through validation, explanation,
or support. But even when we diligently follow instructions,
no lasting change occurs.

Why do we find ourselves caught in this "self-help" cycle,
desperate and alone, when we are trying so hard to improve
ourselves? We sometimes become so frustrated that we
internalize our failures and blame ourselves for not
changing. When we feel this way, our discomfort increases.
Unconsciously we press "replay" on an internal tape
recorder, repeating "I am a failure" over and over again. In
reality, the failure lies not with us, but with the lack of information we need to heal ourselves. We have learned to focus
our energy on the wound, rather than on what caused it.
Like most people who participate in therapeutic practice
and workshops, we mistakenly believe that our problem
falls into one or more of the following three categories:

1) NEGATIVE THINKING AND FEELINGS

2) POOR RELATIONSHIPS

3) DESTRUCTIVE ADDICTIONS, OBSESSIONS
   AND COMPULSIONS

Problems in the THINKING AND FEELING area are usually nagging and painful thoughts and feelings, such as persistent fear, worry, anxiety, hopelessness and helplessness. These conditions are typically accompanied by continuous self-deprecation and disapproval. A typical example from one of our workshops is the following:

Susan R., thirty-six, a free-lance writer and housewife with two young children, feels her husband is always critical of her. "Even though he doesn't criticize me outright, I can tell by the way he looks at me that he doesn't like the way I take care of the children, or how I manage my business. I constantly feel anxious—afraid that I might make a mistake." When we investigated further, we found that these domestic situations were not the only occasions that left Susan feeling anxious and afraid. She experienced similar emotional responses when publishers made constructive comments about her writing and a business friend suggested a different approach to customers. Susan instantly interpreted such professional and friendly advice to mean that she was doing something wrong, and worried about her future performance for weeks and months to come.

Glen W. came in complaining of frequent negative thoughts and feelings that dominated his life. We noticed that Glen constantly put himself down in subtle ways. Upon meeting someone for the first time, Glen immediately began comparing himself with his new acquaintance. The process had become unconscious but the results were concrete; Glen consistently found the other person brighter and more engaging than himself. Because he spent all of his energy sizing people up and worrying about his own performance, Glen lost his own "lustre" and had actually become dull and lifeless. His negative thoughts and feelings kept him from revealing an interesting, even dynamic, inner self.

Negative thoughts and feelings are not restricted to those still searching for their strengths and talents. In spite of her excellent ability as a photographer, Abby remained in a tedious, low-paying job at a branch of an instant-photo company. She spent the majority of her time developing other people's work. Despite many offers to exhibit her own photographs, Abby always found excuses. She was paralyzed by the fear that a public exhibition would reveal what she had always known—that she was a fraud as an artist, devoid of any real talent.

The inability to find or sustain healthy RELATION-SHIPS is another category of problems plaguing our society. Many people experience one failed love relationship after another, or none at all. Personal or work relationships are often hostile, confusing and dissatisfying. When people experience recurring problems with relationships, their lives are characterized by frequent job changes, personal failures, frustration and loneliness.

The case of Fred T., a twenty-six-year-old construction worker, illustrates how problems with relationships can effect the quality of life on many different levels.

Fred has left three different jobs in the last two years because he felt "uncomfortable." "I must be doing something wrong," he said. "Even though I think I'm being friendly to my co-workers, they seem disinterested. They actually try to avoid me. When they see me coming they either walk away or appear deeply engaged in their work." Fred's feelings of personal inadequacy led him to feel rejected by his co-workers. They, in turn, misinterpreted his suspicious attitude and maintained a safe distance. After a short time, Fred would become frustrated, change jobs, and repeat the "uncomfortable" pattern in a new environment. He never stayed anywhere long enough to establish friendships at work, much less relationships outside the construction site.

The third category of problems is equally prevalent in our society. Destructive ADDICTIONS, OBSESSIONS AND COMPULSIONS involve drinking, drugging, eating, gambling, working, spending, sex, hurtful and/or abusive relationships, among dozens of other behaviors. These are often easy to disguise, as we will see in the case of Paul J., a highly paid executive for a luggage corporation.

It seemed like everything was going well for Paul. He had an excellent job, a family he cared about and a respected position in the community. Despite his apparent success, Paul dug himself deeper and deeper in debt every month. He felt unable to stop spending money. He bought all the latest gadgets for the kitchen, piles of toys for the kids and stacks of extra towels, shirts and handkerchiefs. His life was consumed by an over-powering need to buy things either for himself, his family or his friends. In spite of his high income, bankruptcy loomed. Paul's wife persuaded him to seek help after she discovered dozens of Ralph Lauren polo shirts, still in their original plastic wrappers, stashed in their backyard garden shed.

No matter what Greg L. promised himself, he always became involved in relationships with women who "...treat me like dirt. My heart's been broken more times than I can count, but I can't seem to stop finding these kind of women." Greg interpreted this cycle to mean that he was an unworthy, unlovable person. He failed to see that his obsession kept him from forming real, loving associations with women.

After her experience with her first husband, Laurie N. swore she'd never be with a man who hit her. But, no matter how hard she scrutinized prospective partners, relationships always ended in physical abuse.

We mistakenly believe that negative THOUGHTS AND FEELINGS, difficulties with RELATIONSHIPS, and ADDICTIONS, OBSESSIONS AND COMPULSIONS are the problems to be solved because we are consumed by their pain. Although our problems are very real, they are actually symptoms of a deeper situation. Identifying these symptoms as the cause, unfortunately allows the hurt to recur again and again. This way of thinking prevents us from addressing the real problem.

Society teaches us to believe that our symptoms are the real problem. For example, people typically make statements such as: "My problem is that I can't find a satisfying relationship," or "I don't like myself." This type of thinking is too often reinforced by those in the helping professions, who also define the problem in this way. Since birth, we have been taught to believe that the problem, so defined, is what hurts.

The real problem is that we are cut off from our centers, the authentic selves that define us as human beings. When we are not centered, we are not being ourselves. This lack of center is the true cause of our pain, and the key factor in eradicating it forever. The false self that we present to others and are tempted to define as who we are has separated from the inner, authentic self. When we cut ourselves off from this self, we compromise our entire being. The diagram below will help you visualize the relationship between the false, outer self and the authentic, inner self.

Authentic Self

The square in the center represents the authentic self. The squares surrounding it are the layers of "stuff" burying the real you. These layers are the external self. In the following example, notice how the authentic self is hidden by an accumulation of negative feelings and false assumptions.

When Jane W. began therapy, she was so accustomed to

living according to imaginary social standards that she had lost any sense of her own needs. Jane's problem surfaced shortly after she started dating Douglas, a caring, fun-loving photographer. Several months passed before Douglas realized that he had been planning all of their dates and asked Jane what she would like to do that evening. As usual, anything was fine with Jane. When Douglas pressed her for an opinion, Jane sincerely couldn't come up with an idea. Trying to think of something made her increasingly anxious. Douglas was concerned that this passivity might become a potential problem in their relationship; he didn't always want to be in charge. So he began asking Jane questions. At first she was confused, but after talking with Douglas and thinking about her past experiences, Jane realized that she had been cut off from the part of her with clear wants and strong views for many years.

Jane was flooded with sadness as she remembered all the times in her life that she had denied her own interests, opinions and desires in order to please others. She wanted to be liked by people, not make waves. If Jane had been connected to her center during her first marriage, she would have pursued her deepest dreams of becoming a mother and an artist, even though those goals might have created marital conflicts. In her attempt to be selfless, Jane actually succumbed to making life choices that kept her from becoming a fulfilled, successful human being.

When we are in touch with our authentic selves, we feel peaceful, clear and focused. The pieces of our lives are integrated into a unified, purposeful whole. We instinctively know how to move through life with power and success. The principle of consciously connecting has been central to all the great world religions for thousands of years. Prayer, chanting and meditation are methods of making this connection.

We are born as authentic selves. From earliest childhood, we adapt to social ideas and expectations in order to feel loved and accepted. This social need motivates everyone. Children unconsciously abandon their real selves in order to secure love and acceptance vital to their being. By the time we reach adulthood, most of us are unfamiliar with our true selves, and therefore, well acquainted with pain and emptiness.

As the preceding examples have shown, we constantly seek ways to relieve our pain. Psychotherapists and authors of self-help books promote "sure-fire" solutions for solving personal problems and proclaim guaranteed methods of living life to its fullest. We are given techniques that instruct us in finding satisfying relationships, or increasing self-esteem and confidence, with the promise that our problems will simply disappear. Although such techniques can be useful, they are limited and incomplete. Some do work for short periods of time. However, as you have probably discovered, they don't work permanently because they fail to address the root cause of our problems.

Groups like Alcoholics and Overeaters Anonymous offer support and encouragement for kicking addictions as they teach us how to restructure our lives. Unfortunately, such groups also reinforce the notion that there will always be something wrong with us. We are trained to believe that our core is addicted to a negative habit or behavior. This is accomplished through exercises that force us to identify ourselves in terms of our symptoms. For example, "My name is ......, and I am an alcoholic." "My name is ...., and I am a bulimic." This recovery model defines us as victims for life, ignoring our ability to reconnect to the enormous power and love of the authentic self. Although this approach may successfully arrest our addiction, it doesn't teach us how to get centered and remain connected for the rest of our lives. We may have all the techniques and explanations for our symptoms, but if we fail to address the lack of connection to the authentic self, we will endlessly struggle with our symptomatic problems. The lost connection is at the root of all our problems.

When we first experimented with the concept of Conscious Connection, we had serious doubts about the validity of our discovery. The concept seemed too simple, and it contradicted fundamental principles that we had been trained to believe. It was difficult to let go of our familiar ways of thinking, even though years of study and successful practice demonstrated the power of Conscious Connection. We were still reluctant to present our work in book form. Our hesitancy to accept our proven results is similar to that of clients who have recently learned about the Conscious Connection Exercise; in both cases, time and effort must be spent unlearning ineffective methods of therapy. As we opened our minds to the potential of our discovery, we became more and more excited about using

Conscious Connection with our clients. Soon they were actively confirming that this simple, effective method of achieving inner peace worked.

Early on in our research, we were inspired by the work of author, researcher and M.I.T. Professor Thomas Kuhn. In his extensive research on the methodology of scientific research, Kuhn discovered that scientists often strongly resist new discoveries that are inconsistent with their previous knowledge. If a new idea emerges inconsistent with an established scientific view or paradigm, scientists go to great lengths to keep from adjusting their thinking. Kuhn's work in the scientific community parallels our experience in the field of psychotherapy. Clients have difficulty releasing old ideas and beliefs in favor of new ones, even in the face of overwhelming evidence that the old paradigms are ineffective.

This book does not offer a standard psychological approach to the solution of problems. Our method was developed as a result of frustration with the traditional plan of attack. Instead of directing our effort at curing symptoms, we developed an exercise for focusing energy on the authentic self. Through this process, clients gain more and more control over themselves; as a result, troublesome thinking and feeling, problems with relationships and addictions, obsessions and compulsions diminish. Life is full of challenges. The process of Conscious Connection gives you the emotional equipment necessary to meet them.

How do we know if we are cut off from our center? The following quiz will help determine whether or not you are centered. Use it as a reference tool whenever you feel troubled by relationships, addictions, obsessions and compulsions or thoughts and feelings. The questions will remind you of the undeniable link between your "problems" and not being centered.

Begin a notebook now, and in it write down those questions to which you answered "yes." You will find this a helpful companion as you go through the book.

---

1. Do you often feel sad or anxious for no apparent reason?
2. Do you sometimes feel like your life could spin out of control?
3. Do you ever feel like you might go crazy?
4. Are you plagued by worry?
5. Do you consistently feel people try to manipulate or put the screws to you?
6. Do you frequently feel stuck or taken for granted in your job or relationships?
7. Do you feel like you have to prove yourself all the time?
8. Do you often feel like you need to try harder?
9. Do you feel like your life is the same old unfulfilling thing day after day?
10. Do you often feel disconnected or anxious when you are with others?
11. Do you generally feel uncomfortable being alone?
12. Do you feel consumed with jealousy at times?
13. Do you often feel betrayed by others?
14. Do you often feel lonely even when you are with other people?
15. Do you often feel unfocused or without direction?
16. Do you frequently feel numb or dead inside?

If you honestly answered "no" to all the questions, then you are centered and do not need this book. If you answered "yes" to even one question, centering is a problem, and the Conscious Connection Exercise could change your life.

Maybe you've been aware of "off-centered" feelings, but haven't understood where they came from, why you have them, or what to do about them. You feel powerless to rid yourself of the pain. These feelings are what we call *counter-connected*. This is the state of being "not centered." In this disconnected, uncertain state, you are particularly vulnerable to emotional stress.

If you answered "yes" to either question 1, 2, 5, or 13, your *counter-connection*[SM] could be triggered in the following way. Imagine you came home and found that you had been burglarized. Someone had gone through all your personal things, doors and drawers were open, papers and clothes were strewn about. Some of your most cherished possessions were gone. How would you feel? Feelings of anger, depression, anxiety, helplessness and violation are natural after such a traumatic experience.

But, if these feelings remained very powerful, even after you'd done everything possible to retrieve your stolen things and taken precautions for the future, then you would be stuck in a *counter-connection*. Questions 1, 2, 5, and 13 address these disturbing feelings and reflect your "off-centeredness." Given the circumstances, these feelings are understandable. The problem is not in having the feelings for a short period of time, but in allowing them to overwhelm your life.

When any feelings like (anger, depression, anxiety, help-lessness or fear):

- remain very strong
- no longer have a logical relationship to an external event
- become pervasive

you are *counter-connected*—locked into a negative state of feeling and thinking. As a result, you might find a familiar critical voice taking over, constantly belittling your every thought and action, creating persistent fear, worry, anxiety, hopelessness and/or helplessness. Or, you may experience trouble forming successful personal and work relationships. In spite of all your efforts, they are unsatisfying, painful, confusing and short-lived. You may also experience ongoing problems with compulsive drinking, eating, drugs, gambling, work and hurtful or abusive relationships.

Let's return to the burglary example. Of course, anyone would feel violated or fearful in this situation, but why are some people able to move on while others are paralyzed by their fear?

Most of us live with a negative state, our *counter-connection*. It is not our authentic self, but our false self, easily brought to life when difficulties strike. In the burglary example, the *counter-connection* was triggered by a situation that should not have caused serious long-term emotional stress. When this happens, it then serves as "proof" of a pre-existing belief, such as:

"I don't deserve to be happy and fulfilled."

"When good things happen in my life, they never last."

"Life is not worth living."

"I will not do something unless I can do it perfectly."

"If I let myself get close to someone, they might leave me and I could not survive the hurt."

These beliefs pull us away from our centers because they sustain a negative frame of mind, stirring our *counter-connections* into action. Lurking in the background, unyielding to reason, these negative beliefs block out rational thinking. The *counter-connection* takes charge with its own prescribed set of responses. As a result, all events fit neatly into our distorted view of the world. We find ourselves blind to any means of escape. Obviously, such a negative state of being consistently affects our relationships with others and shapes the way we live our lives. Though we may learn to understand why these feelings developed, it still seems impossible to make the changes we know are good for us.

When real or imagined events set off our *counter-connection*, our rational mind temporarily stops working. Like a volcano, we erupt with destructive symptoms in three areas:

1) THINKING AND FEELING

2) RELATIONSHIPS

3) ADDICTIONS/OBSESSIONS AND COMPULSIONS

As we have seen, feelings of *counter-connection* take on a

life of their own. In the same way, symptoms can become blown out of proportion and prevent us from living stable lives. If pain is pervasive, immediate, and intense, we feel compelled to find relief. At this stage, we are sucked into a repetitive cycle of relief attempts because we've failed to attack the real problem. As our efforts increase, the root of the pain is only further obscured. We find ourselves hopelessly locked into a "quick-fix band-aid mentality." Damaging symptoms will continue to pervade our lives until we change this limited approach to resolving our problems.

Because this thinking is so ingrained, it may require a leap of faith to accept the importance of consciously connecting with our centers. It may be difficult to believe that reaching the authentic self gives us the inner strength, inner knowledge, and clarity of thought necessary to see our problems differently. Our new resources, the product of Conscious Connection, will allow us to confront those once insurmountable problems and to arrive at resolutions we never could have imagined in our previous emotional state. We have nothing to lose by learning to re-connect. We have everything to gain.

At birth, we are naturally connected to our authentic selves, our birthright. The late Abraham Maslow, a psychologist famed for his innovative research on the positive healthy aspects of the personality, has studied moments in the human experience that resemble our original state of connection. These "peak experiences" are " . . . moments of pure, positive happiness, when all doubts, all fears, all inhibitions, all tensions, all weaknesses, were left behind. All separateness and distance from the world disappeared." Maslow's description of these peak experiences is similar to the experience of Connection. However, although Maslow was fascinated by these moments, he regarded them as rare, spontaneous and accidental. We have found that, if given the proper tools, we can re-create these moments at will with the same incredible results that so intrigued Maslow.

The Conscious Connection Exercise is the tool that enables us to return to our centers at will. Countless clients report that when they deliberately connect, they achieve a clarity, calm and inner strength that empowers them to successfully handle situations that had previously overwhelmed them.

There are four aspects to the Conscious Connection Exercise:

■ Focused attention

■ Relaxation

■ Imagery

■ Refractionation

Focused attention involves directing your attention onto one thing as you screen out any distractions. It is a basic principle of any inner-directed practice in which the goal is to guide or control the mind. When the mind is distracted, mental energy is diffused. By disciplining the mind, we will learn to direct our concentrated mental energy on a single object. Our mental powers work according to the principles of contemporary physics; combinations of thoughts, feelings and imagery produce powerful electromagnetic energy, which creates a magnetic field acting like a magnet to the outside world. The magnet attracts equivalent energy. What we produce on the inside is replicated on the outside. For example, if we consistently imagine frightening situations, we unwittingly attract precisely those situations. On the other hand, the reverse is also true. If we consistently expect the best and visualize positive images, we manifest love in our lives. The success of Conscious Connection depends, in part, on maximum concentrated energy.

The first part of the exercise will relax you so that maximum focus and concentration can occur. Relaxation techniques date back to the 1930's, when psychophysiologist Dr. Edmund Jacobson showed that muscle tension is directly related to anxiety levels. When muscles are tense and anxiety is high, the brain is deprived of oxygen-rich blood. As muscle tension is reduced and emotional anxiety subsides, the brain is bathed in blood. Our brains need the maximum oxygen in blood to think clearly.

Imagery focuses the attention further by helping us develop a vivid, three-dimensional image that incorporates all of our senses. When we develop this detailed picture, the brain cannot distinguish between image and reality. Therefore, we have the power to change our present experience by replacing negative thoughts and feelings with our positive image.

The fourth aspect of the Conscious Connection Exercise is refractionation, a technique used in hypnosis to deepen an instruction to the mind. Through the use of refractionation techniques, we learn to recall and trigger experiential pictures (the three-dimensional image you developed using relaxation) at will. Refractionation, or repetition of the centering exercise, embeds the experience in the mental landscape. This image—our Conscious Connection—takes us back to our centers whenever we choose. The energy focused on the authentic self overcomes the false external self. Our Conscious Connection replaces our *counter-connection.*

The following examples from our practices and personal lives will give you an idea of the many different ways people arrive at their Conscious Connection.

JOY: *When I was seven, I remember it was Halloween night and I wore an incredible witch costume that my mother had made. It was truly extraordinary. I could feel and smell the cool crisp Montana air of Fall. I ran from house to house trick-or-treating with my friends. It was exhilarating. The feeling that came to my mind was FREE.*

Then when I stayed with the feeling, another image came to me. I saw myself galloping down a dirt path in the woods in perfect harmony with my horse, Penny. We were flying through the air. I felt absolutely no fear, in fact, I felt extraordinarily SAFE. It was wonderful. Nothing could stop me.

Since Joy had two images, we suggested that she experiment with both for a few days until a single image seemed to dominate.

SHERRY: *I go back to the birthing room of my second*

grandchild. I had been with my son and daughter-in-law throughout the seventeen hours of labor. We were totally immersed in the experience. The sounds in the room were almost inaudible, as if coming from a great distance. A few minutes after she was born, my daughter-in-law gave me the baby to hold. I'll never forget the overwhelming love I felt for Nicole as I held her tightly to me. I felt euphoric. The one word that encompasses all my feelings was LOVE.

JIM: *I went home to visit my folks last Easter and went to church with them Easter morning. As I walked in, I heard the ringing of bells, smelled burning incense, and saw streams of colored lights pouring in through the stained glass windows. I was overcome by a powerful sense of REVERENCE and CALM. I felt as PEACEFUL as I ever had.*

FRAN: *When I sprinkle magic dust over me, I feel great! I see myself walking in a beautiful valley. I am walking straight and tall with immense confidence. There are snow-capped mountains in the distance, the air is crisp with the scent of lilac and heather. I feel the sun and a mild wind as I move. Even though I hear animal sounds, there is the sense of a very PEACEFUL QUIET. At that moment I get it. I want to hold onto that feeling of CLARITY.*

We see from these examples how each individual creates his or her own personal connection. Because it is not mechanical, artificial or imposed from the outside, the

Conscious Connection is inherently strong. It is a natural process that can be experienced at will. Now it is time for you to discover your personal connection. Find a quiet place where you will not be disturbed for several minutes. Later, you might want to tape record this and listen to it anytime you wish as you are learning to Consciously Connect.

Sit back and close your eyes for a moment.

Take three deep breaths, and with each breath release any tension you are holding.

Imagine the sun above your head shining its warm golden light down upon you.

Allow every muscle in your body to relax as you feel this warm light washing over you.   *(pause)*

Imagine you have some magic dust.

Sprinkle it over yourself.

Imagine you have the power to feel any way you want.

You may have felt this way before. If so, recreate that feeling. If not, allow the dust to spontaneously create this feeling for you now.   *(pause)*

Choose a meaningful word or words that describe this feeling.

See yourself connected to your authentic self.   *(pause)*

Focus in on your image.
     See the details . . .
     Hear the sounds . . .
     Savor any smells or fragrances . . .
     Let yourself experience all the sensations that are part of
     your picture as you connect to your authentic self.

Take a long moment and let this experience saturate your being.
(pause)

As you open your eyes, continue to consciously experience your image and feeling.

NOW . . . TAKE THREE DEEP BREATHS AND . . .

Close your eyes again. Imagine you have a movie camera.

Sharply focus in on your centering experience and all of its
details.   *(pause)*

Run your movie in your mind now. This is what you will do
whenever you want to be centered.

In your notebook, write down the words and sensory
impressions from your Conscious Connection experience.
This list of reminders will allow you to re-create your centering experience quickly and easily.

WORD(S)

FEELINGS

SOUNDS

SMELLS

OTHER SENSATIONS

COMPOSITE VISUAL IMAGE

Without continual practice, your Conscious Connection
will fade and your *counter-connection* will take over. After
frequent repetition however, getting in touch with your
Conscious Connection will become automatic. In our professional workshops and seminars, we have found that the
mind and body learn through repetitive, concrete action.
Remember when you learned to ride a bike or drive a car?
At first, it felt awkward and unnatural. You had to think
about what to do next. But the more you did it, the easier it
became, until you didn't even have to think about it. You
could just enjoy the experience. Conscious Connection
becomes an automatic process in the same way. Let's do it

again:

RELAX: Take three deep breaths and visualize the golden light washing over you.

RECALL: Your FEELINGS, SOUNDS, SMELLS, MEANINGFUL WORDS and VISUAL IMAGE

BE: Connected to your authentic self.

Sheila, one of our clients, has been a student of Conscious Connection for several months. She is a hospital nurse and feels that one of the doctors she works for treats her unfairly. Sheila experiences feelings of personal humiliation, insecurity and hostility in response to his gruff and demanding manner. Sheila believes that the doctor takes her for granted and manipulates her in carefully calculated ways. These feelings trigger her *counter-connection,* an overriding sense of powerlessness, an all too familiar feeling Sheila has carried around with her for many years.

Locked into her *counter-connection,* Sheila either reacts like a hurt little girl or delivers a sarcastic retort. In the past, she felt she had been honest about her feelings, but the doctor always seemed defensive and disinterested.

One day the doctor burst into a room where Sheila was with a patient.

"Sheila, where the hell did you put yesterday's charts?" he demanded.

Sheila remembered returning the charts to their proper place. He just hadn't looked. The false accusation in the presence of a patient was more than she could stand. She felt the familiar fury rise up. But, before replying with her usual sharp wisecrack, Sheila reminded herself of the Conscious Connection Exercise she practiced every morning. She excused herself to the patient and walked into the next room. Sheila had already decided that she wanted to end up feeling different this time, regardless of the doctor's response.

Sheila RELAXED, took three deep breaths and visualized the golden light washing over her. She RECALLED her connection, seeing herself down by a river bed, smelling the freshness of the air, and hearing the water rush in front of her. Almost instantly, Sheila felt CALM. With each moment, her feeling of strength grew. She felt a connection (BE) with her authentic self. Now she understood that she didn't have to participate in the doctor's anger or feel the pain that came with it. Once Sheila decided how she wanted to think, act and feel, whatever was at the root of his anger became meaningless. She could choose how to respond. No longer stuck in her *counter-connection*, Sheila recognized the doctor's anxiety, the reason now being unimportant. She returned to the room.

"You sound upset. How can I help you?" she asked, gently.

The tension immediately left the doctor's face.

"I'm sorry," he said. "I've just had a very upsetting argument with my son."

For the first time, Sheila and the doctor understood each other's feelings.

This was just one of Sheila's many positive experiences

after she began practicing Conscious Connection. Instead of feeling victimized in her relationships, she became increasingly powerful in effecting the outcome of difficult situations. We watched in awe as the real Sheila emerged, self-confident and full of life, a natural leader.

Now you pick a personal situation that is currently uncomfortable and unsettling. Re-connect with your authentic self by using the three step process: 1 RELAX, 2 RECALL and 3 BE.

From this connected place, re-play the difficult situation in your mind. When you are in this positive state, your connection acts as a filter and automatically screens out your *counter-connection*. Ask yourself the difficult questions that you have been avoiding: "How do I want to handle the situation? How will I feel about myself once I take action?"

This is the ideal technique to use when you have the opportunity to step back from problematic situations. As you use Conscious Connection more frequently, you will learn to invoke it on the spot. Conscious Connection will become your automatic response to emotional stress.

We cannot leave the trap until we know we are in it.

AQUARIAN CONSPIRACY

Two

UNMASKING THE VILLAIN:
COUNTER-CONNECTION

THE following conversation took place during Cory's participation in a workshop:

CORY: *I can't stop helping people.*

SHERRY: *What's so bad about that?*

CORY: *There's no end to it; I'm so busy helping everyone else that there is no time left for me.*

SHERRY: *How does that feel?*

CORY: *Awful.*

As she said this, her shoulders slumped and her eyes filled with tears.

FRAN: *It looks like you're feeling sad too.*

She nodded.

FRAN: *When do you first remember feeling this way?*

CORY: *As long as I can remember. Mom was always counting on me to take care of my little sisters.*

FRAN: *That must have been a big responsibility.*

CORY: *Yes. It felt like I really didn't matter. It seemed like Mom expected me to forget about myself and to do only what my sisters wanted.*

SHERRY: *And what went on in your head when you were feeling sad?*

CORY: *I guess I thought I was never going to get what I wanted.*

By the time Cory was eight years old, she had made up her mind that she "wasn't going to have what she wanted," and at twenty-eight she still believes it. This convoluted thinking compels Cory to help everyone else, even though her obsessive pattern of self-sacrifice makes her an unhappy person. In her "free" time, Cory takes home-cooked meals to a widower and spends weekends watching a friend's children. She also volunteers for Planned Parenthood and participates in the Big Sister Program. But rather than complement her busy life, Cory's many activities mask feelings of personal insecurity. She often feels the familiar emptiness and sadness that was so much a part of her growing up. She does not know how to give herself the love and care that she needs. Cory's negative belief coupled with ever-present feelings of sadness, lock her into her *counter-connection*. This upside-down thinking-feeling alliance still overwhelms her life even though it no longer matches present day reality.

Until your *counter-connections* are made conscious, they are involuntary responses triggered by any stimuli that your mind associates with earlier painful experiences. Anything you see, hear, sense, or even imagine can trigger an old alliance and, without your realizing it, control your present behavior. The case of Susan W., forty-one, a college history professor, illustrates this point. One evening, Susan attended a party for new faculty members at the university, and became engaged in discussion with a colleague. After a few minutes of animated conversation, the colleague unexpectedly ended the talk with "We'll have to discuss that more later," and walked away. Susan immediately wondered what she had done to chase her friend away. Was she too aggressive with her questions? Did she seem carried away by her enthusiasm? Susan spent the rest of the party in a corner of the room, considering a long list of possible offenses. Her formidable scowl intimidated the new teachers and kept all but the very bravest from approaching her.

If Susan had been thinking logically, she would have realized that the colleague had no intention to slight her, but simply wanted to mingle with other guests at the party. Unfortunately, Susan's response to such situations had become automatic. After interviewing Susan, the root of her problem was discovered. Susan's mother suffered from chronic depression. When Susan was at the developmental stage of believing that everything in the world was about her, she decided it was her job to make her mother happy. Unable to succeed, young Susan came to the conclusion that she must be doing something wrong. To this day, the belief formed from her childhood failure often returns when Susan feels vulnerable. She ignores her adult resources and reacts as if she were still six, the age at which this painful, confusing relationship was originally experienced. Susan's reaction is a typical human response to a traumatic childhood experience.

Because these negative, unconscious decisions are at the core of our *counter-connections,* it is critical to understand exactly how they came to be, what they are, and how they influence our lives. A destructive, yet seemingly insignificant or meaningless pattern of behavior that seems unrelated to our problem, may be the product of our *counter-connection.* For example:

Bill's *counter-connection* is triggered whenever his girlfriend seems to be enjoying herself with other people. Even though he tells himself he's being ridiculous, Bill is sure she will like them better than him, feels scared, and concludes he's not lovable. As a result, Bill frequently cuts off his girlfriend in the middle of her conversations, interrupts others and delivers rude jokes. His loud, obnoxious behavior masks his internal panic, and drives his girlfriend away.

Karen is thrown into her *counter-connection* whenever she perceives anyone being critical of her. She feels hurt and devalued, believing that no matter what she does or says, it will never be enough. It's not easy for Karen to be in any relationship, work or personal, without pressuring herself to be perfect.

Joe experiences frustration and sadness whenever

anyone at work is promoted, even if it has nothing to do with him. His belief that other people are able to get what they want, but he is not, overrides his good sense. Because Joe wears his sadness on his sleeve, his failure to move up at work becomes a self-fulfilling prophecy. No one is inclined to promote someone who is down all the time.

By repeating a belief over and over to ourselves, often unconsciously, we become convinced of its absolute, unalterable truth. This repetition is a form of brainwashing, and it becomes the script to which our lives conform. Karl Pribram, a well-known neurophysiologist, discovered that the brain does not distinguish between what is real and what is not; it accepts every bit of information it is fed. Thus, what we believe becomes our reality.

The case of George L., a forty-year-old accountant, shows how *counter-connections* can be passed on by family members, affecting the lives of several generations. George's father was meek and passive. Because he felt unable to stand up to his wife, he allowed her to make most of his career and personal decisions. George spent his early years watching Dad cower as Mom laid down the law: "You can't set foot outside until you fix that banging in the radiator again! Why don't you ever do anything right the first time!" By age nine, George had internalized the *counter-connection* of feeling powerless and believed he was incapable of running his own life. Since George had no practice or confidence in his own decision-making abilities, any major decision and even some minor ones, triggered his *counter-connection*. He felt paralyzed. Rather than risk making a mistake, he did nothing.

It's no surprise that, despite feeling unappreciated, George has remained in the same unhappy work situation for thirty years. He derives no sense of purpose from his job. Although George is desperate to change his life, his *counter-connection* always stops him from taking any initiative. Even when new job possibilities fall into his lap, George finds himself unable to pursue a course of action. Feelings of powerlessness cause him to lapse into his *counter-connection*. Like his nine-year-old self, George thinks, "I won't measure up. I can't do it." As a result, he fails to see opportunities when they arise and discourages himself from making any real changes in his life.

Counter-connections control behavior. In George's case, anyone expressing an opinion contrary to his wears Mom's face. He makes them an instant authority, accedes to their point of view and feels like a powerless child. George was shocked when he realized that his present life is controlled by the thinking of a nine-year-old. As he learned more about *counter-connection*, it became clear to him how his pulled him off-center and prevented him from taking charge of his life.

George recognized that his "yes" answers on the "Are You Centered? Quiz" related to his *counter-connection*. His affirmative response to "I often feel sad or anxious for no apparent reason" reminded him of solitary hours spent lying on his bed wondering what to do next. Rather than attempt to fulfill his hopes and desires, George frequently remained "stuck in jobs and relationships," and experienced life as "the same old unfulfilling thing day after day." The Conscious Connection Exercise helped George begin to act forty (his real age) instead of nine. As he learned to consciously connect to his center, George felt more and more confident. Over time, he made more decisions on his own and became less afraid of making mistakes. Encouraged by his success, George practiced centering and increasingly took positive action on his own behalf, recognizing that current problems were really symptoms of being off-center.

Patsy S., forty-seven, provides us with another example. Patsy's *counter-connection* sprang from what she assumed her parents expected of her, and her desire to please them. They considered the arts hobbies and equated academics with real success. Patsy's twin sister, Jill, excelled academically with minimal effort, but Patsy had to work hard for good grades. By junior high, it was evident that Patsy's true talent was in dance and music. Once, when Patsy tried to enroll in an after school dance class, her Mother grounded her for a week. Schoolwork was too important to waste time leaping about in tights and a tutu. Even when the school band instructor spoke with her parents about renting a band instrument, they remained unmoved; school was a place to read and write, not toot a horn. Because she felt she could never measure up to Jill's academic achievements and her parent's high expectations, Patsy decided that something was wrong with her. No matter what she did, she felt inadequate. This thinking-feeling alliance, her *counter-connection*, created a pall over her life.

Years later, Jill attended medical school and established

herself as a prominent surgeon, while Patsy struggled through law school before finally becoming a lawyer. Dance and music remained her real love; the less she participated in them, the more off-center and unhappy she became. Because Patsy wasn't doing what she loved, a constant nagging sadness pervaded her life. It never dawned on her that she had bought into her parents' value system and remained trapped by it. Although she is an independent adult free to form her own judgements, Patsy found herself behaving as if she were still a schoolgirl.

When Patsy learned Conscious Connection, she reconnected to her center and felt free to be herself. She saw her life from a different perspective. Being a lawyer was for her family. Dance was for her. Patsy knew she was old to be a professional dancer, but it was not too late to dance. She found a local dance company, tried out and made it. She felt great! Eventually Patsy planned to become involved in choreography. She still practiced law, but now it was only a small part of her life. Most important, Patsy had allowed herself to make choices based on her wishes, not those of her parents.

As the cases of Cory, George and Patsy have shown, *counter-connected* thoughts and feelings are at the core of our anguish. When these strike, they are powerful, and we only want relief. What can we do to rid ourselves of such terrible, pervasive feelings forever? Recognizing that we are experiencing *counter-connected* feelings is the first step toward getting permanent relief and ultimately taking control of our lives.

How do we form *counter-connections*? At any point in time, we are vulnerable to negative influences, particularly if they are repetitive and/or traumatic. As a result, we construct on the spot, specific, illogical and negative beliefs about ourselves and the world that both structure our thinking and determine the way we feel.

Questions from the "Are You Centered? Quiz," such as "Do you often feel lonely even when you are with other people?" and "Do you frequently feel numb or dead inside?" helped Peter face how lonely and empty he felt. He had been feeling unhappy for so long that he could hardly imagine a different state of being. Even though Peter had achieved success in some areas of his life, loneliness and emptiness overshadowed any good feelings these successes brought. After years of feeling unable to have a mutually loving and trusting relationship, Peter doubted he could ever become close to a woman. In desperation, he decided to seek help.

When Peter came into therapy, he was asked about his problem. He said, "I want a relationship, but I either haven't found the right person or something is wrong with me." When pressed further, Peter revealed that he wouldn't let himself think about beginning another relationship. He was afraid of being disappointed, as he had been so many times in the past.

Peter talked about a woman named Susan. After acknowledging that they got along well on most levels, Peter admitted that he was irritated when she was five or ten minutes late. Even though they shared mutual interests and physical attraction, Peter could not forgive Susan's habitual lateness. At first, it was difficult for him to understand that her lateness was an insignificant ingredient in an otherwise good relationship. Several therapy sessions passed before Peter realized that his thinking was irrational, and agreed that something inside him must have created such a strong reaction.

Peter said that when he was four years old his mother was hospitalized several times over a year for treatment of a chronic illness. Each time she left, he felt abandoned—terrified that she might never return. Peter's fears were perfectly reasonable for a boy his age, whose world revolves around a primary caretaker. The thought of reliving that childhood pain was so scary that young Peter decided it was too risky to get close to anyone; they might leave at any moment, just as Mother had. As he grew into an adult, Peter's fear of the old pain created a protective wall around his authentic self. There was no way he would allow himself to be hurt again.

The pattern was always the same. Every time he approached intimacy, his childhood belief, "It hurts too much to love anyone. They might leave me," was triggered. Consumed with fear, Peter would run. Unconsciously, he continually reinforced both his belief and his feelings by either choosing someone equally afraid of intimacy, or by finding a reason to end the relationship before the other person could leave. In this way, Peter unwittingly sentenced himself to a lifetime of loneliness.

Peter spoke about his last relationship, a summer romance with a paralegal named Carol. He recalled that frequently, after what he thought was a long stretch of feeling good together, Carol would suddenly become consumed with work and unwilling to see him for days at a time. When this happened, Peter felt confused, lonely, and yet, oddly relieved. Before he began practicing Conscious Connection, Peter blamed Carol for refusing to get close. After connecting with his authentic self, he began to see how both of them unconsciously colluded to maintain the emotional distance that prevented a close relationship. Once it was pointed out that this behavior sabotaged his relationships, and that he and Carol shared a mutual problem, Peter understood how he contributed to his feelings of loneliness and emptiness.

Peter was astounded when he realized that he was avoiding close relationships by insulating himself from re-experiencing the devastating pain he felt as a young child. Despite this realization, Peter did not understand how his adult resources, his ability to think independently and clearly, could help him overcome his problem. Peter is not alone in reacting as if he were still four years old. Most of us do this quite often.

As we have seen, Peter began therapy thinking that his problem was his inability to stay in a relationship. The Conscious Connection Exercise helped him discover that he was off-center, living defensively with the goal of avoiding any hurt or fear. Peter was unconsciously programming himself to feel lonely and sad. His heart would stay closed as long as he was in this upside-down, *counter-connected* state. Locked into the results of a childhood fear, he didn't have a chance at a healthy relationship. Peter had no idea that his *counter-connection* was running his life until he got connected. Once he was centered, Peter was able to get beneath his *counter-connected* outer layers of negative "stuff." He could then feel the security, calm and rationality of his authentic self.

When he connected to his center, Peter immediately felt an amazing transformation taking place within himself. The empty hole inside began to fill with contentment, like the honey in Winnie-the-Pooh's pot. He laughed, remembering the security of that childhood image.

Peter connected by imagining himself hiking in the Sierras. He faced even the most treacherous, ice-covered peaks without fear. This was a place where he felt secure and confident in his ability to conquer any challenges. Peter's rational mind took control, telling him that if he could climb a mountain, he could change the way he thought and felt. In this state, Peter could see clearly. He had deprived himself of closeness for too long.

Shortly after he learned the Conscious Connection Exercise, Peter met Lynn. His old fears immediately resurfaced. But, rather than spiraling into his *counter-connection* and sabotaging the relationship, Peter immediately used the Conscious Connection Exercise to contact and release his authentic self. This allowed him to shift his energy away from the old negative pattern and focus it on specific positive thoughts and feelings. As a result, his *counter-connection* (negative thinking and feelings) was automatically screened out. For the first time, Peter did not pull back. He told himself that no matter what happened with Lynn, he would remain in touch with his confident, authentic self. No longer paralyzed by helplessness, Peter reported that "taking chances, and experiencing closeness, beats loneliness any day."

Peter's case demonstrates the transformation brought about through Conscious Connection. His struggle with negative thoughts and feelings is a typical example of a *counter-connection*. His belief that abandonment might occur at any moment was reinforced by feelings of loneliness and emptiness; the result was a *counter-connection* so powerful that Peter believed he could never change. Remember, in a *counter-connection*, feelings are very strong, pervasive, and no longer logically related to an external event.

Because our negative decisions determine the way we live, preventing us from staying connected to our centers and consistently interfering with the quality of our lives, we must learn to understand and eliminate them. Often our *counter-connected* beliefs result from experiences over which we had no control, like those of childhood. A four-year-old can be emotionally and physically devastated when a parent isn't there to take care of him, as was Peter, but an adult isn't dependent in the same way. Although we cannot alter the past, we can change the present. Either we choose to remain victims by repeating our negative decisions, beliefs and feelings over and over again, or we revise our thinking so that it improves our lives today.

At different times in our childhood development, we think in terms of black and white, see ourselves as the center of the universe, and think concretely rather than abstractly. Our distorted perception often leads to faulty interpretations. For example, all parents of small children know that no matter how much time they spend with their children, from the child's point of view, it is rarely enough. In most families today, it is necessary for both parents to work to either meet financial demands or realize personal goals. Unfortunately, in the developmental stage of "black and white thinking," a child might interpret this situation to mean that her parents would rather work than be with her, not at all her parents' intent. At the stage when a child sees everything as revolving around her, and her parents are often away working, she might become confused about her parents' purpose, decide something is wrong with her, and feel abandoned. Throughout our lives, it is not uncommon for all of us to make these kinds of distorted decisions about ourselves and the world. Problems emerge with how we idiosyncratically interpret our experiences based on our unique natures and stage of growth.

Not all *counter-connections* are as long-standing and destructive as the preceding examples. Sara's life up to the age of thirty-seven had been fulfilling. Her job as a manager for a commuter airline was fast-paced and suited her outgoing personality. Sara felt able to handle life's challenges as they came along. But, after nearly seventeen years with the same airline, Sara was ready for a career change. She decided to accept a job as a consultant for a large corporation that was experiencing administrative difficulties. Although she liked her co-workers and found the work rewarding, Sara became increasingly unhappy at her new job. Try as she might, Sara couldn't shake her depression. She decided to try therapy for the first time in her life.

In the first session, Sara talked about her experiences in her previous job and her current situation. It was clear that Sara's "career change" was not solely based on wanting a different kind of job. Her last boss at the airline was demeaning, oppressive and rigid. Although she constantly felt humiliated, she kept trying to please him. For almost two years, Sara spent several hours every day hoping he would change. The unrealistic demands continued. Finally, Sara convinced herself that she needed some excitement in her professional life, a rationalization that gave her the courage to quit.

At her new job, Sara suffered a daily barrage of demands and criticisms from her supervisor. Since she had just started, Sara thought her complaints might be justified. Based on past experiences with people in authority, Sara believed criticism did not come without good reason. Once again, she concluded that it was up to her to try harder. Instead of realizing that both bosses were unreasonable, Sara convinced herself that she was the problem. Nothing she did would ever be enough; as a result she felt anxious and unhappy. This negative state became her *counter-connection*.

The only way out of her unhappiness was to either change her reaction to her bosses or to change employment. The more Sara practiced connecting to her authentic self, the more confident she became about her own competency.

By the third and final session, Sara felt her old self again. She accepted a new job as manager of a software business, and soon discovered her talent for helping others gain confidence and fulfillment in the workplace. In the future, Sara trusted that the moment she felt consumed by the need to try harder, she would know she had allowed herself to be pulled off-center. If this happened, her work would be to get back on track by consciously connecting. From that perspective, she would be in a much better position to assess the situation and take action that would maintain her connection.

Remember the "Are You Connected? Quiz" on Page 30? Any question you answered "yes" to indicates that you are off-center—stuck in *counter-connected* feelings and faulty thinking. For example, in the question, "Do you feel consumed with jealousy at times?," the key word is "consumed." When jealousy overwhelms and preoccupies us, controlling our lives, we feel anxious, fearful, unhappy, and constantly vigilant. Like a virus, feelings of jealousy and mistrust have a toxic effect on our relationships, infecting them with suspicion and animosity and creating polarization between us and other people. As others move farther away from us, we feel increasingly anxious, fearful and unhappy, and thus the negative thinking-feeling cycle is reinforced.

Pick the question you answered "yes" to that affects your life the most. Replay in your mind the worst thing that has already happened or could happen when you feel this way. Really focus in on it. Picture all its details. Describe it out loud, allowing yourself to feel its intensity for the next few minutes.

We know how difficult it is to confront your worst fears. Don't feel discouraged or afraid of these bad feelings; they are valuable because they signal something is wrong. Whether moderate or tremendously strong, negative feelings indicate that we are off-center and provide the first step in the process of re-connecting to our authentic selves.

Let's review the diagram depicting the authentic self:

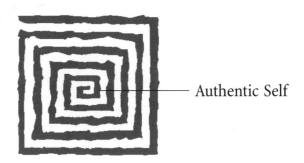 —— Authentic Self

When you're not centered, you are not living from your authentic self. The essential part of you we talked about in Chapter One is buried under layers of "stuff." These layers, your *counter-connections*, are composed of the defenses you've developed to protect yourself from pain. Think of the *counter-connection* as the encapsulation of all your lingering painful memories from the past, the experiences you have interpreted negatively that continue to control your life.

Despite this interfering stuff, your authentic self remains intact and can be readily accessed. Recall how you feel when you are consciously connected to your center by doing the Conscious Connection exercise now.

RELAX: Take three deep breaths and visualize golden light washing over you . . .

RECALL: Your FEELINGS, SOUNDS, SMELLS, MEANINGFUL WORDS, and VISUAL IMAGE

BE: Connected to your authentic self.

Notice how different you feel from when you were *counter-connected.* As if by magic, the bad feelings disappear. Nothing mystical is going on. You're just not used to how it feels when you take active control of your thoughts and feelings.

However, since this is the first time your *counter-connection* has been challenged, there's going to be a battle. By repeatedly consciously connecting along with changing your negative thought patterns, you will have the ammunition you need to wage war against your *counter-connection.* The more often you practice getting centered by consciously connecting, the stronger your authentic self will become. The obstructive layers that you use to protect yourself will eventually atrophy from lack of use. Over time, consciously connecting along with your new beliefs will allow you to be your loving, powerful self every single day.

Before we become familiar with a new city, we expend much time and effort reading maps, understanding directions, and recognizing landmarks. After living in one place for awhile, we no longer need such guides. We become so comfortable that we even forget about the difficult period of adjustment. The streets and neighborhoods, once a confusing maze, now have familiar names and associations. At first, you may not see a direct way to your authentic self, but once you experience a **conscious connection**, you will know that the path is clearly marked.

Authentic Self

A divided disconnected self

We become what we think about all day long.

RALPH WALDO EMERSON

Three

COUNTER-CONNECTED
THINKING

THERE'S a certain amount of validity to the nutrition-ist's adage "you are what you eat," even as we imagine human twinkies and hamburgers with arms and legs. But what about the "food" that we feed our minds? Perhaps our most incredible human power is the ability to decide what to believe—the capacity to determine our own emotional realities. As we have seen in the preceding case studies, beliefs and feelings continually reinforce one another, sticking together like crazy-glue. Our beliefs make us feel a certain way, and feeling that way strengthens what we believe. Feelings of anger, depression, anxiety, or helpless-

ness that remain very strong, no longer have a logical relationship to an external event, or become pervasive are
always associated with negative beliefs. The force of this
negative combination spirals us into our *counter-connection,*
and we find our lives controlled by a negative thinking and
feeling partnership. We are trapped in defensive living.

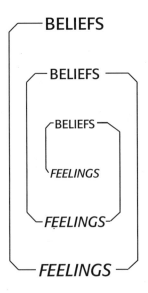

The following statements will help you uncover the
unconscious beliefs that influence your life. Even statements
that are only partially true influence thinking and, therefore,
need to be identified. The questions may not represent all of
your beliefs. As you discover more about yourself, you will
become aware of more beliefs to add to your list.

BELIEFS INVENTORY

WRITE IN YOUR NOTEBOOK ANY OF THE FOLLOWING STATEMENTS THAT ARE TRUE BASED ON YOUR IMMEDIATE RESPONSE. IF THERE IS ANY TRUTH TO THE STATEMENT, RECORD IT.

---

1. I sometimes think I am a bad person.
2. I am not lovable.
3. I do not deserve to be happy and fulfilled.
4. I am not important.
5. No matter what I do or how I do it, it is not enough.
6. Often, when I get what I want, I do not feel satisfied.
7. I will not allow myself to be happy and fulfilled if it makes someone close to me feel threatened.

8. When good things happen in my life, they never last.
9. I cannot overcome the negative effects of my heredity, past experiences, and relationships with people.
10. Someone or something often prevents me from getting what I want.
11. Others are able to get what they want, but not I.
12. I do not have enough time, money, talent or freedom to do what I want.
13. It is not possible for me to change.

In Questions 15-18, we are defining "struggle" not as a dynamic challenge, but as something frustrating, laborious and relentless.

14. Most of the time I experience life as painful.
15. Daily struggle makes me a better person.
16. Everything worthwhile requires a long struggle.
17. Life is a struggle.
18. If there were no struggle, I might get bored.

19. I will not do something unless I can do it perfectly.
20. If I do something that is less than perfect, I feel upset.

21. If I get close to someone, I might lose myself.
22. If I let myself get close to someone, they might leave me and I could not survive the hurt.

Put your answers aside for a few minutes. We will be going back to them soon.

Do you sometimes wonder why, when you go after something you really want you don't get it? The answer lies in your beliefs. When our unconscious negative beliefs conflict with our desires, the powerful negative beliefs always win the battle. In the following example, Sherry explains how this dynamic operated in her life.

I was participating in a professional seminar that met bi-monthly. The purpose of the group was to explore the efficacy of various therapeutic methods of treatment. From the very beginning, one of the participants pushed my buttons constantly. It seemed as though Meg always wanted to be the center of attention; she consistently interrupted other people and refused to consider their opinions, much less their individual needs. Everyone attending the seminar had a different area of expertise, and I really wanted to hear the ideas of some of the other participants. But whenever anyone started to share, Meg managed to shift the discussion in her direction. Each time this happened, my stomach began to ache. I felt jumpy, frustrated and helpless. From my experience with Conscious Connection, I knew that one of the ways I feel when I am not connected is helpless, my *counter-connection.* I also realized that in order to change my bad feeling, I had to identify its partner, the controlling belief. It was hard not to blame Meg for monopolizing the seminar, and to admit that my belief was interfering with the experience I desired with the group. Thanks to my training in Conscious Connection, I discovered the culprit.

Underlying my helplessness and frustration with Meg was the belief, "I am not important." I had decided this as a young child. Whenever my mother was upset by my behavior, my father insisted that I apologize. Often I saw the situation differently. Why should I apologize for something that was not entirely my fault? But, no matter how well I argued my position, my father insisted that I apologize. As a result, I grew to believe that my feelings were unimportant and felt helpless to change this reality. My *counter-connection* surfaced in stressful situations, such as in the conflict with Meg in my seminar. Like Peter in the last chapter, I felt like a child, helpless and without options. As an adult, I know this is the last thing my father would have wanted me to think. His only intent was to make my mother happy, and I, unbeknownst to him, misinterpreted his insistence that I apologize to mean I was not important.

As soon as I realized that I was operating from childhood thinking, I consciously connected and felt powerful and clear. Once I accepted that I could not alter Meg's behavior in the seminar, the responsibility shifted back to me. All the energy I had been expending blaming her was now available to help me change my thinking. I focused this energy on a new belief, "I am important. I count." Although her behavior didn't change in the least, as soon as I stopped blaming her, I felt empowered. I was no longer frustrated and helpless. I had choices.

Without making anyone the guilty party, I could bring the issue up openly in the group of having time for everyone to talk, and find out if the other participants shared my perception. If so, we could discuss how we might develop a better way to hear one another. If not, I could either stay in the group and decide that I would be satisfied with whatever benefit I derived, or I could simply leave the group and find one more to my liking. By connecting to my authentic self and changing my thinking, I successfully broke my *counter-connection* spiral.

Before we discuss moving beyond negative beliefs, we need to further examine how such beliefs develop and influence your life.

What we think determines our perspective of life. Although our beliefs play this major role in our lives, they are actually nothing more than conclusions we come to in our own heads, positive or negative. Beliefs are based on our interpretation of situations, traumatic or pleasant, and/or repetitive childhood experiences. As Muriel James and Dorothy Jongeward point out in *Born to Win*, we form most of the beliefs that constitute our concepts of self-worth and the worth of others by the age of eight. From an adult standpoint, many of these beliefs are unrealistic, distorted and irrational. Nevertheless, they determine the roles we play in life and how we play them.

Understanding the origins of our beliefs allows us to

change our perspective. First, we need to realize the significant difference between who we are now, and who we were when we made the decisions that currently guide our lives. Obviously, we have far more resources and experiences to draw upon now than we ever did as children. However, we are so used to thinking and acting according to our old beliefs that it may require a leap of faith to convince us of our adult power to change.

Beliefs originate in how we interpret messages—verbal or non-verbal communications we received from people we valued highly, or from religious and educational institutions. Cultural mores can sometimes be even more insidious than messages communicated from individuals, and trap us as effectively. From early childhood, we unconsciously accept our society's view of things. We are socialized to adhere to that view, creating upside-down thinking, getting further away from our own inner truth. Even if we become aware that our truth is in conflict with that of our culture, the pressure to agree is so great and the anxiety created by the cognitive dissonance so uncomfortable, that we often feel we have no choice but to conform.

Our interpretations of messages from our environment trigger a belief/decision that in turn evoke feelings. This occurs as we translate the message into experience, even though our interpretation (especially when it occurred in early childhood) may or may not have anything to do with the original intent of the communicator. This combination of messages, beliefs and feelings is a powerful alliance that becomes our *counter-connections*. It's that simple.

Notice the way messages, decisions and feelings led to Brenda's *counter-connections*, a client of Fran's. The more you observe the process in action and apply it to your own life, the faster you defuse the power of your negative beliefs.

BELIEF 1: *I am not lovable.*

When I was a little girl, my parents had a Fourth of July party every year. My Mom always bought me a new dress and spent a lot of time fixing my hair. She said everyone would notice how pretty I looked. It was true. I did get a lot of attention from the guests. Naturally, I thought they noticed me because I looked pretty. From this experience, I assumed that people will only notice me for how I look (Message). I decided that I am not loveable (Belief/Decision) and felt very sad and empty (Feeling).

BELIEF 2: *No matter what I do or how I do it, it is not enough.*

Regardless of what I achieved as a small child, it seemed to me that my father always found a way to diminish the accomplishment. Whenever I brought a project home from school that I thought was great, he pointed out how it could be improved. It became clear to me that I would never be good enough (Message). I decided "No matter what I do or how I do it, it is not enough" (Belief/Decision) and felt hurt and empty (Feeling).

BELIEF 3: *When good things occur in my life,*
they do not last.

What I remember most vividly about my mother is a statement she repeated often, "After laughter, come tears." She never seemed to be joyful when good things happened. Once when I was in high school, I won an internship with a theater group. It was a dream come true for me, but when I rushed home to tell Mom, she just shook her head and warned me about getting too excited. She was sure I would fall behind in my schoolwork or make mistakes in the upcoming production. From her response, I learned that "It is better to stay emotionally neutral than to suffer the disappointment that inevitably follows something good" (Message). Her words were like a black cloud that constantly hung over me. I decided that "When good things occur in my life, they do not last" (Belief/Decision). I felt confused and scared (Feeling) whenever something good happened. Rather than risk the pain of possible failure, I decided not to accept that high school internship.

As a result of the beliefs outlined above, Brenda consistently has problems in her relationships with men. Her adult behavior corresponds with the message-belief/decision-feeling pattern established in her childhood. Sometimes, Brenda picks a man like David, who has no intention of leaving his wife, although he professes adoration and attraction to Brenda. At first she felt excited and hopeful even though she was well aware of his marital status. As she got more involved and David showed no desire to leave his wife, Brenda became increasingly sad and empty, acting clingy whenever she was with him. David couldn't understand her changed behavior; he hadn't changed.

In the short time she spent with Joseph, Brenda became obsessed with making everything perfect, an impossible task for anyone. Brenda spent hours folding clothes and making the bed; even the slightest wrinkle in a sheet would cause her to tear off the bedding in frustration and start over. Joseph was frightened away by her bizarre behavior. Brenda's fear of happiness ended many potential relationships. After a spectacular date with Robert, Brenda convinced herself that the good feeling could never last. She became increasingly insecure, calling him several times throughout the day. Robert was a writer who needed peace and quiet to concentrate on his work. The relationship was doomed even before it began.

Brenda's relationships were not threatened by her appearance, personality or principles, but by beliefs she internalized as a small child. She feels hurt and empty most of the time. Her thinking reinforces her feelings, continually spiraling her into the *counter-connections* that are the very root of her problem. Until she frees herself from her powerful controlling negative beliefs, Brenda is trapped in an internal battle she cannot win.

In freeing yourself from your negative beliefs, it is important to distinguish between the beliefs you maintain as opinions and those you hold as convictions. You can tell the difference between the two by the degree of emotional and/or intellectual resistance you experience when confronting data that runs counter to your beliefs. With convictions, you justify, rationalize, or discount any new information that is contradictory, and even wage internal battles to maintain your beliefs. You feel far less defensive about your opinions.

The following examples show the difference between an opinion and a conviction. Both cases illustrate the negative influence of an old, unexamined belief. In the first example, notice how quickly Leslie is able to come to terms with a long-standing opinion. The second example illustrates how much difficulty David has in even acknowledging that he is under the sway of a powerful conviction.

Leslie S., twenty-nine, is a first generation Chinese-American. In her culture, children are expected to take care of their parents throughout their lives, even if it requires great sacrifice. While participating in a group therapy session, Leslie mentioned that her parents were in serious financial trouble. Although they had the ability to work and had property they could sell, they expected that their children should be the ones to sacrifice. They demanded that Leslie come up with the money to bail them out. She had already given them all her savings the last time they needed help, and was barely able to pay her own rent. Leslie found herself consumed with guilt over her failure to obtain the necessary money.

The group helped Leslie explore her beliefs about parent/child relationships. It became clear that Leslie had adopted the cultural more that children should take care of their parents under any circumstances. When asked to think about this cultural expectation in terms of her own beliefs, she began to question its validity. Leslie believed that members of a family should be supportive of one another, but not to the point of taking care of those who could take care of themselves.

"I feel so guilty about believing this," Leslie said. "How can I not feel guilty?" she asked. The group was supportive, affirming that Leslie is her own person and has a right to think for herself. Group members suggested that whenever she feels guilty, she remind herself that it is okay for her to think differently from her parents and that she is not to blame for their troubles. The tension immediately began to drain from Leslie's face. She needed the group to affirm what she suspected was true. Leslie said she felt confident that she could release herself from her inhibiting opinion. Because she was dealing with an opinion, not a conviction, Leslie remained open to new information, saw that she could have a different view from her parents, and took action that felt right for her.

Convictions are more difficult to overcome. When you find yourself justifying and rationalizing one of your beliefs, and discounting anything that disproves it, you are protecting a conviction. Since convictions differ from opinions in intensity and in the hold that they have over us, they require special handling. You can remove beliefs that are opinions by gaining new information. However, convictions are deeply embedded, and require reprogramming to be permanently changed (discussed in Chapter Four).

David L., a dentist, had the belief (conviction), "I am not

lovable." Although he yearned to have a fulfilling relationship with a woman, David simply could not accept that someone might actually love him. He found all sorts of ways to discount any evidence of love and care. As a result, his relationships inexplicably fell apart—or so it seemed to him. In a session with Fran, the dynamics became clear.

> DENNIS: *I've met a lovely lady. Laura seems to think everything about me is okay. She's considerate. She does whatever she says she's going to do. I think I like her.*
> FRAN: *Sounds great!*
> DENNIS: *You won't believe this. Last week was my birthday, and Laura insisted that we celebrate. She surprised me with an incredible evening and paid for the whole thing. As if this weren't enough, she gave me the most extraordinary gift. Laura knows that I collect rare books and that I've been searching for one in particular. Somehow she found it and bought it for me. No one has ever done anything like that for me before.*
> FRAN: *It sounds like she really cares for you.*
> DENNIS: *(Incredulously) Nah . . . she's just an exceptional person. I'm sure she's this way with everyone.*

Although David's belief (conviction), "I am not lovable," was formed in early childhood, it continues to plague him as an adult. He fears getting close to a woman because of his certainty that sooner or later, she will discover that he is not worthy of love. As a result, David ends relationships before that can happen.

David's conviction will remain intact as long as he protects it by discounting and rationalizing anyone's interest in him. Until he acknowledges the enormous power that his conviction has in shaping his intimate relationships, and reprograms his belief, his relationships are destined to fail.

Refer back to your BELIEFS INVENTORY. If you answered "True" to any of the questions, negative beliefs are shaping your life. This will sound discouraging until you understand that you are not your beliefs. Once you become aware of how you think, you can change your thinking so that you are no longer at the mercy of negative beliefs. No matter how powerful your beliefs may be, you are more powerful. You can learn to move beyond them by identifying what they are and where they come from. The following exercise will help you unravel the sources of your formative messages, feelings and decisions. In the next chapter, you'll learn how to change them.

Go back to the BELIEFS INVENTORY on page 69. For each statement you answered TRUE, ask yourself the following questions. Write your answers in your notebook.

---

1. When do I first remember thinking this way?
   Who was there? What was happening? What did I think was being said? (Message)
2. What did I decide about myself, others, or life as a result? (Belief/Decisions)
3. What did I feel? (Feeling)

There is a feeling that comes directly on the heels of the interpreted message. Notice how this same feeling becomes intensified and embedded after the belief/decison is made.

In Chapter Two we talked about the negative decisions we make as children and as adults. Because our decisions significantly affect the way we live, it is important that we learn to understand and eliminate the beliefs that comprise our *counter-connection.* Unfortunately, we cling to these beliefs as if they were life preservers. We feel safer holding onto something familiar than letting go and discovering what life would be like without it. Does this strike you as irrational? Wouldn't we want to let go of something that isn't good for us? Of course we would—if we were operating from an adult perspective. However, when it comes to our deep-seated beliefs, we react with the part of us that is still a scared and inexperienced child. Because children equate familiarity with security, the child in us panics when it comes to giving up beliefs. This instinct is so powerful that a child will actually choose to live with a familiar abusive parent rather than an unfamiliar non-abusive person. All rationality is put aside when we are faced with the prospect of losing anything we consider essential to our security, such as our beliefs.

The mind accepts programming in various ways. We are all accustomed to the conditioning that comes from parental figures—parents, teachers, older siblings, grandparents, or virtually anyone who had an impact on our development. Cultural and religious programming, although not as discernable, can be just as powerful. The programs we chose as a youngster are now guiding and influencing our adult lives. Think about it. Your life today is based on decisions you made with the limited experiences and resources of a young child. Conscious Connection helps bring your limiting childhood beliefs to your adult awareness, allowing you to use your mature experience to reach your true self.

Judy is forty-two. Until recently, she believed that she did not deserve to be happy and fulfilled. Judy's bad feelings about herself caused her to seek approval from other people. She needed constant reassurances that she was really okay. In order to be liked, she attempted to anticipate people's wants, ignoring her own thoughts and feelings. The result of her automatic programming was that she allowed her needs to go unnoticed and she then felt resentful, helpless, and frustrated, which further reinforced her low self-esteem. When Judy uncovered the beliefs that governed her *counter-connection,* she was willing to change them. She was able to make her Conscious Connection through the following dialogue with Fran:

FRAN: *Close your eyes. Relax. Take three deep breaths and think of a time when you felt in touch with your heart, your soul, your center . . . in sync with the best part of you.*
JILL: *Ok, I've got it.*
FRAN: *Tell me about it.*
JILL: *I came home from school, and my Dad was*

drunk again. After pleading with my family, I got
them to finally admit that his drinking was a
problem we had to face together. I felt really clear
and powerful.
FRAN: *How can you best encapsulate that experience*
in your mind?
JILL: *I'm not sure.*
FRAN: *Some people like to form a mental picture.*
Some think in terms of symbols or metaphors. Others
just feel it. You decide what is best for you.
JILL: *Oh, I see what you mean . . . I can just say*
"Power" to myself and the feeling is there.
FRAN: *Great! That's it. Now as you go about your*
daily life, keep that word in the forefront of your
awareness. Focus on it when you find yourself in
uncomfortable situations.

To Judy's amazement, as she practiced this technique,
she felt powerful, centered and clear. She trusted her own
inner processes. Just by imagining and focusing on the word
"Power," and the feelings of strength and clarity it evoked,
Judy made her connection a reality. She practiced connecting every day—in the morning when she awoke, while she
was jogging, and at night before she went to bed. Whenever
she could, she closed her eyes and allowed herself to be
enveloped by the feelings of strength and clarity that
defined her sense of power.

An opportunity soon arose for Judy to actively shift
from her *counter-connection* to Conscious Connection. She

had signed up for a weekend growth seminar with the understanding that it was up to her to determine the fee she could afford to pay. Midway through the weekend, the instructor made a pitch for additional money, based on how much each participant thought the weekend was worth. He attempted to make people feel guilty by telling them that if they had benefited from the seminar, they would want to contribute more. Judy felt uncomfortable and manipulated. She knew that if she acquiesced, it would be from her need for approval—her *counter-connection* of powerlessness. Instead, Judy chose to **consciously connect**. By going inward, she allowed herself to listen to her true thoughts and feelings.

With her Connection as her guide, Judy felt a sense of power emerge. She realized that she did not need to comply with the request. She calmly and clearly stated to the instructor what was true for her, without making him wrong or herself right. She shared her feelings of discomfort, and her opinion that his request was contrary to the original fee arrangement. Although he disagreed, she held firm. Judy left the seminar with new feelings of power, joy and trust in herself. She was excited by the discovery that she could take charge of her life through Conscious Connection.

Connecting to your inner truth is as easy as turning your attention to it. The results that follow will transform your life. Once you are tuned in to what is going on inside yourself, you will more easily maintain a connection with your true self. The next step in this process, re-programming to eliminate the belief-feeling alliances that comprise your *counter-connection*, will be discussed in Chapter Four.

I have not the shadow of a doubt that any man or woman can achieve what I have, if he or she would make the same effort and cultivate the same hope and faith.

MAHATMA GANDHI

Four

TRANSCENDING YOUR BELIEFS

THE preceding chapters have taught you how to reach your authentic self through Conscious Connection and identify the components of your *counter-connection*. Now that you are familiar with the technique, and the way it can transform your life, we need to look even more closely at the beliefs underlying your *counter-connections*. Our discussion of the difference between opinions and convictions in Chapter Three emphasized the depth and power of beliefs, some of which have been controlling our lives since childhood. In order to transcend these deep-seated beliefs, we must learn a bit about how our minds construct what we know as "reality."

The brain does not distinguish between what we **BELIEVE** to be true and what is actually true. It accepts every bit of information it is fed—true or false, positive or negative. We interpret mental images as **REAL** and embed them in our minds as absolute truth. Our beliefs become our reality. Since our brains interpret truth and fiction as equivalent, it is easy to understand how negative images from childhood, such as *counter-connections*, often remain as potent today as when they first occurred. *Counter-connections* develop without our awareness, and seem to be a natural part of our personalities. As insidiously as brainwashing, the beliefs and feelings that compose our *counter-connections* become the script to which our lives conform.

The power of this mental reality is best illustrated by the work of Karl Pribram, a neurosurgeon, psychologist, and neurophysiologist at Stanford University's College of Medicine. Pribram, known as the Einstein of brain research, has likened the brain's functioning to holography. Holography is a form of lensless photography that produces a three-dimensional, life-like image when a beam of light splits into two parts. When these beams collide on film, they form wave-like patterns. In order to reproduce a holographic image, only a small piece of the original is necessary.

If, as Pribram proposes, our brain is a holographic instrument, the images we envision are holographic in nature. With only partial information, our brain puts together a complete picture. For example, suppose your father hit you frequently when you were young. You might decide that all men are cruel. Throughout this book, we have presented case-studies of adult clients who continue to function from such generalized decisions, even though they now live in a very different situation. When we are trapped in our *counter-connections*, we find ourselves incapable of using our adult experience and knowledge to solve our problems; therefore, we continue to act like defenseless children.

How can we use our mental power to escape from negative "realities?" If we are conscious of what we put into our brains, we have enormous control over our lives. Conscious Connection allows us to provide our mental computers with new up-graded software. The following case-studies illustrate how individual realities—mental holograms—shape life decisions. As you read these examples, think about the negative beliefs that influence your own life.

> **BELIEF:** *Others are able to get what they want, but not me.*

Because Patrick feels ugly and boring, he expects all women to reject him no matter what he does. Even so, he goes to singles' functions with his friends, dreaming that he just might find a girlfriend. Instead of being friendly, he acts aloof. "If I'm cool, they won't notice how I really feel," he thinks. As Patrick tells it, he stands alone, looking at the crowd, hoping someone will approach him. As usual, Patrick ends up not finding anyone. He feels rejected, just as he expected. When his friends meet people, Patrick's sense of failure increases to the point of despair. Now he seldom leaves the house for social events.

BELIEF: *I may feel bored if there is no struggle.*

Lucy, a college sophomore, is in a program that requires many term papers. The assignments are given with plenty of completion time, but Lucy always waits until the very last minute to do them. She stays up all night for several nights before the paper is due, working frenetically to meet her deadline. Exhausted and irritable, Lucy complains about needing more time, and yet gets a major thrill from obsessing about her assignment and then pulling it off under pressure.

> **BELIEF**: *I cannot overcome the negative effects of my heredity, past experiences, and relationships with people.*

There is no doubt that Ginny had a difficult childhood. Her parents shifted between being suffocating to totally ignoring her. She and her brothers were made the scapegoats for all her parents' unhappiness and frustrations as they dumped a constant barrage of criticism and physical punishment. Ginny assumed that her parents didn't love her. Consequently, she never felt loved by anyone. At forty-five, she is still trapped by her upbringing, convinced that her relationships never work because of the severe damage she believes she sustained as a child, and cannot change. As a result, she feels unable to risk getting involved.

After Patrick, Lucy and Ginny identified their beliefs, we asked them to observe the ways their beliefs functioned in their daily lives. They were amazed to discover the subtle, yet pervasive influence of each belief. Patrick realized that he even acted "cool" in the grocery line. He recalled the young woman behind him remarking that their tastes were the same, asking him if he liked to cook. Instead of responding in a friendly way, Patrick dead ended the conversation quickly with a cursory, "Sometimes." At first, Lucy refused to believe that procrastinating was anything more than a bad habit. But after her roommates complained about her "moodiness," Lucy admitted that this problem affected her social life as well. Once Ginny began to think more clearly about her belief, she noticed her cold, unresponsive reaction to friendly overtures. She assumed others were only being friendly out of politeness or pity. Now she began to see that believing relationships were impossible caused her to act and think in ways that reinforced this mental "reality."

A core belief is like the trunk of a tree from which other beliefs extend out like branches. If it were not for your core beliefs, your other beliefs would not exist. Refer back to the BELIEFS INVENTORY in Chapter Three. Notice that it is divided by spaces into five separate groups, each of which represents a different core belief. The questions are manifestations of the following beliefs:

- Group 1–7: **I AM NOT OK THE WAY I AM.**
- Group 8–13: **I AM NOT IN CHARGE OF MY LIFE.**
- Group 14–18: **LIFE IS PAINFUL.**
- Group 19–20: **I AM NOT OK UNLESS I AM PERFECT.**
- Group 21–22: **IT IS TOO RISKY TO BE VULNERABLE.**

When Patrick thought "Others are able to get what they want, but not me," he was operating out of his core belief, I AM NOT IN CHARGE OF MY LIFE. Lucy's desire for excitement and attention resulted from her conviction, "I may feel bored if there is no struggle," a manifestation of LIFE IS PAINFUL. Sometimes it is hard to convince yourself that ordinary behavior is the result of a core belief. How could a "personality trait" like procrastination reflect an attitude toward life? We used the following exercises to help Patrick, Lucy and Ginny understand the powerful, pervasive nature of their core beliefs.

- Practice observing your beliefs by watching, without criticism or judgement, how they operate in every aspect of your life. You will begin to see that all individual beliefs actually emanate from the five basic core beliefs.

- Once you have isolated your beliefs by category, spend several days watching each belief manifest itself in your life. How does a belief affect your behavior? What are the ramifications of your actions?

- Trace your core beliefs from their roots to the "branches" that govern your daily activities.

Become aware of how you create your own self-fulfilling prophecies. Even the most intelligent, introspective people find themselves reinforcing the same negative thoughts and behaviors over and over again. We unwittingly revise our experiences, and/or set up situations that produce the same feeling state as our *counter-connections. Counter-connections* automatically program behavior; if you are unhappy, you make sure you stay that way. When your *counter-connection* is operative, it is a driving force, the lens through which you view life and literally perceive everything that happens. But, despite their power, *counter-connections* are not indestructible.

By getting Consciously Connected and changing your beliefs, you eliminate your *counter-connections.* Observe how this happens in the following example of Fran's client, Nancy. First, Fran helps Nancy identify her *counter-connection* feeling state. Following the process in Chapter Three, they probe the origin of one belief Nancy listed on her BELIEFS INVENTORY, so that she can identify the original message connected to her belief, her feelings at the time, and the decision she made.

FRAN: *When you don't feel good inside, what do you feel?*
NANCY: *I feel empty and helpless.*
FRAN: *Is that how you feel when you think that no matter what you do or how you do it, it is not enough?*
NANCY: *Yes.*

FRAN: *When do you first remember thinking this way? Who was there and what was happening? What do you think was being said?*

NANCY: *When I was around six or seven, my mother really had a lot of trouble coping. She'd tell me life was not worth living. Sometimes she stayed in bed all day long. Other times she rushed around cleaning the house, as if preparing for visitors. I was scared that she was going crazy. I would have done anything to make her better.*

FRAN: *What did this mean to you?*

NANCY: *It meant that it was my job to make Mom happy so that she would know that life is worth living. (Message) I promised to be good and make her happy. But, no matter what I did, Mom never got better.*

FRAN: *What did you tell yourself?*

NANCY: *I told myself that something was wrong with me because I couldn't make Mom happy. I thought if I tried harder, then maybe I'd help her.*

FRAN: *So you decided that no matter what you did or how you did it, it was not enough (Decision) and you just felt —*

NANCY: *Helpless. (Feeling)*

FRAN: *Right. That is your counter-connection. How does this play out in your life right now?*

NANCY: *It seems that no matter what I do, I can't make it with men. I just can't seem to please them.*

Further discussion revealed that Nancy chose men who had been unhappy for a long time and who looked to her for self-fulfillment. Obviously, nothing that Nancy did could ever be enough because their misery had nothing to do with her in the first place. Fran pursued the subject through Nancy's relationship with her current boyfriend, Kenneth.

FRAN: *Tell me about a time that left you feeling as if you hadn't done "enough" for Ken.*
NANCY: *That's easy. Just yesterday, I felt lousy all day, like maybe I was coming down with the flu. But after work, Ken called and said that he had a tough day. He had nothing to eat at his place, and asked if he could come over. What I really wanted to do was crawl into bed, but I pretended to be cheery and sympathetic. "Of course," I said, "I'll make you dinner." I scrambled around and put together a really nice meal. Everything was ready by the time he arrived. Right after dinner, he said he was in a bad mood and went home. He never acknowledged my effort or even recognized how lousy I felt.*
FRAN: *How did you feel then?*
NANCY: *Much worse. Awful. Just like I used to with Mom.*
FRAN: *Exactly! You feel this way in your relationships because you are reacting like your six-year-old self. That core belief is still controlling your life, even though it doesn't match up with your current reality and truth.*

NANCY: *I get it . . . I've been acting as if I were still six.*

FRAN: *Right! And still feeling helpless. Would you like to change that?*

NANCY: *Absolutely! But how? I try every day. I just don't know what more to do.*

FRAN: *Whenever you're involved with a man and you begin to feel helpless, it's a tip off that you might be plugging into your old program. Remember, that little six-year-old did what she thought she had to do at the time, based on the resources available to a little girl. Ask yourself if you are thinking, feeling and behaving the way you did when you were six. Are you trying to please? If so, you can decide that you are a grown woman and can respond in a different, more appropriate way.*

Fran then explained a series of exercises that helped Nancy eliminate her negative core belief. The steps she used apply to all of us. Adapt them to your particular beliefs and situations.

---

1) You no longer need to protect yourself as you did when you were a small child. Remind yourself that you are grownup. Tell your small child self that she (he) is lovable just the way she (he) is.

2) Implant in your mind the belief that what you do is enough, simply because you are lovable. You are unique. There is only one of you in the whole world. Notice how this contradicts your destructive belief. Believing in your own special nature is a very different way of being in the world. Don't

waste your energy struggling with the old belief. Focus on the new one.

3) Practice implanting your new belief as often as possible. Do this as you **Consciously Connect** with your authentic self.

In Nancy's case, Conscious Connection is feeling love for herself. In the past, her image of herself was as a vulnerable, sad and helpless little girl. As she repeats her Conscious Connection word, love, she embraces and loves that little girl. Nancy sees a transformation come over her; her little girl is safe, and she is a strong, capable adult.

TRUE answers to any of the questions on your BELIEFS INVENTORY mean that you are susceptible to slipping into your *counter-connection* just like Nancy. But take heart! Our research and experience have shown that

NO BELIEF IS SO POWERFUL THAT IT CANNOT BE CHANGED THROUGH IMPLANTING A NEW, POSITIVE BELIEF. TO SUMMARIZE:

■ **IMPLANT POSITIVE BELIEFS IN YOUR MIND**

■ **ALLOW OLD, NEGATIVE BELIEFS TO EXIST SIMULTANEOUSLY**

■ **IMAGINE AND ACT ON NEW BELIEFS AS IF THEY WERE ALREADY TRUE, PRACTICING THEM IN TANDEM WITH YOUR CONSCIOUS CONNECTION**

Sherry's client Dennis provides us with another example of how a *counter-connection* can be successfully identified and transformed. Dennis felt separate from everyone. No matter how much anyone loved him, he still felt alone. From Dennis's BELIEFS INVENTORY, Sherry knew that three of his beliefs were:

1. I am not lovable.

2. I am not important.

3. If I let myself get close to someone, I might get hurt.

Based on her knowledge of Dennis' beliefs, Sherry initiated the following discussion.

SHERRY: *You've been talking a lot about feeling disconnected from others. Try this. Ask yourself how you would like to feel instead of disconnected.*

DENNIS: *Easy. I'd like to feel connected.*

SHERRY: *I call that feeling of "disconnected" a counterconnection. It's easy to identify from your BELIEFS INVENTORY. If you think you are unimportant and unlovable, how could you feel anything but alone and apart? If you think it is unsafe to get close to anyone, you won't even try. How did you feel when you were little, living with your father? What did you say to yourself when he hit you and finally left?*

DENNIS: *I felt miserable—totally unloved, unwanted, alone and worthless. (Feeling) I remember saying to myself, "Something must be really wrong with me." (Message)*

SHERRY: *When your father walked out, you thought*

that you must not be important enough or lovable enough for him to stay. And because this hurt so badly, you decided that it was just too risky to get close to anyone. (Decision) That decision is still operating in your life even though Dad is no longer a threat.

DENNIS: *Right. So how do I get out of it?*

SHERRY: *Remember the work we did around Conscious Connection? You felt FULFILLED when you sprinkled magic dust over yourself. Your image was of you feeling that way when your child was born. You saw yourself holding your baby minutes after he was born, heard him gurgling, saw him looking up at you. You felt overwhelming love and joy filling your whole body. Now, get connected and keep your connection at the forefront of your mind.*

Then, (Step One) tell that little boy inside of you that it is okay to feel all feelings. You won't be devastated no matter how bad they feel, because you know how to take care of yourself today.

Next, (Step Two) affirm that you are lovable and worthwhile just the way you are. Allow this belief to exist alongside your old beliefs. Focus all of your energy on the new belief, without concerning yourself with whether you believe it or not. Your mind will accept what you tell it and create a new context through which to experience the world.

Practice this process, and your Conscious Connection (Step Three), as often as possible.

Finally, (Step Four) give yourself permission to move through this exercise at a comfortable pace. You have stuffed your feelings deep inside for many years, so don't be surprised if they surface in strange and exaggerated ways. You need to get used to these new, positive feelings. Just accept them and know that the strangeness will dissipate over time.

DENNIS: *Boy, I'd like to believe that your system works.*

SHERRY: *Try it.*

Dennis did try it and it did work. He walked around angry and hurt for awhile. He found he had no patience. When the gas station attendant didn't service him immediately, he revved up the engine and roared off in frustration. When a bank clerk made an innocent mistake, Dennis felt overcome by his anger, and inappropriately berated the embarrassed clerk. But even this was reassuring, because at least he was feeling something. After a few weeks, these feelings began to dissipate. Dennis said he "felt lighter." Soon he was experiencing a range of emotions, including love and joy. Because he could now distinguish between his *counter-connection* and his Conscious Connection, Dennis realized that he could choose how to live his life. Once you reprogram how you think, and practice consciously connecting, you will feel more in charge of your life than you ever thought possible. You will find yourself able and eager to resolve even seemingly unsolvable dilemmas.

As you have seen in the examples of Nancy and Dennis,

whenever *messages* form beliefs, *feelings* are triggered automatically. This happens even though your interpretation of a *message* (especially when it occurred in early childhood) may have nothing to do with the original intent of the communicator. The combination of how you interpret *messages* and the *feelings* you internalize as a result, creates a powerful alliance in determining what you *decide* as your basic life beliefs. IT'S THAT SIMPLE.

If what you believe does not get you what you want, you have two choices. You can resign yourself to accepting your fate, or you can decide to take responsibility for your destructive beliefs and direct your energy to beliefs that *will* bring you what you want. For example, take the belief, "If I let myself get close to someone, they might leave me and I could not survive the hurt." Deep down, everyone wants to be close to someone. Yet, as long as you believe you could not survive the possibility of hurt, you will not allow yourself that closeness. The result is a solitary, isolated existence that "feels safe."

On the other hand, try this: along with your belief, "If I let myself get close to someone, they might leave me and I could not survive the hurt," introduce the thought, "Closeness is a gift I give myself and if I get hurt, I am capable of taking care of myself." Can we hold two opposing thoughts at the same time? It is not only possible, but also essential in bringing about the change you desire. The way to break habits is to direct your energy—your thoughts and feelings—to the desired belief, rather than struggling with the old one. It means giving up actively fighting, resisting or negating the old belief and instead, simply allowing it to exist. This is a different process from what most of us are used to, and it works by effecting a vital shift in energy and focus.

When you struggle with a belief, you energize it precisely *because* you are thinking about it. Conversely, if you direct your energy to a new, desired belief, that belief becomes stronger while the undesired one atrophies. All you have to do is focus your concentration on this new belief. The old belief will reside peacefully beside it.

In the course of his extensive research on creativity, Psychiatrist Albert Rothenberg found that creative efforts thrive on the allowance of contradiction. His examples range from playwrights who give their plots and characters dimension through the interplay of antithetical elements to the research of eminent scientists. According to Rothenberg, if Einstein had not allowed opposing theories of physics to coexist in his mind, he could not have accepted and pursued his revolutionary Theory of Relativity. Rothenberg calls this ability to permit the coexistence of black, white and all shades of gray "Janusian thinking." Janus, the Roman god of doorways and beginnings, is often depicted with two faces, one looking forward, the other backward.

Why not look forward with the thought, "Closeness is a gift I give myself and if I get hurt, I am capable of taking care of myself"? While you do this, allow the backward-looking thought, "If I let myself get close to someone, they might leave me and I could not survive the hurt," to simply be. (Of course, substitute whatever opposing thoughts apply in your particular case.) This practice can make even the most mundane events and situations seem like miracles. Take the example of Fran's client, Emily:

Emily's *counter-connection,* "No matter what I do or how I do it, it is not enough," and the feeling of powerlessness, occurs every time she and her mother speak on the telephone. A typical conversation goes like this:

EMILY: *Hi Mom.*

MOM: *Hello dear, how are you doing?*

EMILY: *Pretty good, but right now it's hard to talk, because I've just started feeding the baby. I'll call you back later. (Her mother doesn't respond) What's the matter Mom?*

MOM: *Lately, it seems like there's always something. You never have any time for me anymore.*

EMILY: *Mom, that's not true. I can't help it if the baby is crying. I just talked to you a few days ago and we had a long talk, remember?*

MOM: *Big deal. We talked five minutes.*

EMILY: *Mom, that's just not true, it was more like a half hour. I can't help it if I have a family.*

MOM: *So I'm no longer your family?*

It is all too easy to see Emily's "No matter what I do or how I do it, it is not enough" belief in operation here. While talking to her mother, she slipped into her *counter-connection,* became defensive and tried to prove to her mother that she really is a "good daughter." Frustrated with that approach, she worked on reprogramming her belief and consciously connecting.

As often as she could throughout the day, Emily focused on her new belief, "I am just fine the way I am" and connected to her internal power. She chose "powerful," as her connection word and used it with the image of seeing herself entering a room with nothing in it but a large, very special book. No matter what page she opened to in the book, she always saw the words, "I am just fine the way I am." She immediately felt powerful and trusted her thoughts and feelings. The next time her mother called, the conversation was very different . . .

EMILY: *Hi Mom.*

MOM: *Hello dear, how are you doing?*

EMILY: *Just great, glad you called, but we're just sitting down to breakfast. I'll call you back as soon as we finish.*

MOM: *(Long pause) There's always something more important than me.*

EMILY: *Mom, I really* do *want to talk to you. I'll call you later.*

MOM: *I won't be home.*

EMILY: *All day and all night?*

MOM: *You're not the only one who's busy, you know.*

EMILY: *Mom, I really love you. I'll just keep trying until I get you.*

Emily's mother will continue to be who she is. But when Emily lives from her **Connection**, she experiences her mother very differently. More important still, she no longer has to endure those awful, guilty, powerless feelings. If that is not a self-created miracle, what is?

You too, can create your own miracles by using the following guidelines:

---

1) Take your True answers from your BELIEFS INVENTORY, and for several days, observe how and when they come up in your daily life.

2) Restate the core belief and the belief that emanated from it. Then, rephrase both statements positively. You can use the words we have chosen or, better still, translate them into your own words until they sound and feel right. It's important that the statements ring true for you.

Each person will want to tackle this exercise in his or her own style. There is no one right way. Some will take one belief at a time. Others will deal with the categories of core beliefs. Both approaches work.

The following examples will guide you in transforming your negative beliefs into positive ones. (The beliefs are numbered as they are on the BELIEFS INVENTORY.)

TRANSFORM YOUR NEGATIVE BELIEFS

1. Belief: I often think I am a bad person.

   (Core Belief: *I am not OK the way I am.*)

   Because I am OK the way I am, the bad things I've done are not about who I am.

2. Belief: I am not lovable.

   (Core Belief: *I am not OK the way I am.*)

   Because I am OK the way I am, I am lovable.

3. Belief: I do not deserve to be happy and fulfilled.

   (Core Belief: *I am not OK the way I am.*)

   Because I am OK the way I am, it is my birthright to be happy and fulfilled.

4. Belief: I am not important.

   (Core Belief: *I am not OK the way I am.*)

   Because I am OK the way I am, I am important.

5. Belief: No matter what I do or how I do it, it is not enough.

   (Core Belief: *I am not OK the way I am.*)

   Because I am OK the way I am, no proof is required.

6. Belief: Often, when I get what I want, I do not feel satisfied.

   (Core Belief: *I am not OK the way I am.*)

   Because I am OK the way I am, I love myself and feel fulfilled.

7. Belief: I will not allow myself to be happy and fulfilled if it makes someone close to me feel threatened.

   (Core Belief: *I am not OK the way I am.*)

Because I am OK the way I am, I always have myself to count on.

8. Belief: When good things happen in my life, they never last.

   (Core Belief: *I am not in charge of my life.*)

   Because I am in charge of my life, I can continually make good things happen.

9. Belief: I cannot overcome the negative effects of my heredity, past experiences, and relationships with people.

   (Core Belief: *I am not in charge of my life.*)

   Because I am in charge of my life, I can determine how the past affects my present.

10. Belief: Often, someone or something prevents me from getting what I want.

    (Core Belief: *I am not in charge of my life.*)

    Because I am in charge of my life, I have the power to get what I want.

11. Belief: Others are able to get what they want, but not me.

    (Core Belief: *I am not in charge of my life.*)

    Because I am in charge of my life, I have as much chance of getting what I want as anyone else.

12. Belief: I do not have enough time, money, talent or freedom to do what I want.

    (Core Belief: *I am not in charge of my life.*)

    Because I am in charge of my life, I make the changes I choose.

13. Belief: It is not possible for me to change.

    (Core Belief: *I am not in charge of my life.*)

    Because I am in charge of my life, I make the changes I choose.

14. Belief: Most of the time I experience life as painful.

    (Core Belief: *Life is painful.*)

Because I choose to see life as challenging and dynamic, I embrace its ebb and flow.

15. Belief: Daily struggle makes me a better person.

    (Core Belief: *Life is painful.*)

    Because I choose to see life as challenging and dynamic, I understand what I do is not who I am.

16. Belief: Everything worthwhile requires a struggle.

    (Core Belief: *Life is painful.*)

    Because I choose to see life as challenging and dynamic, I know only my best effort is required.

17. Belief: Life is difficult.

    (Core Belief: *Life is painful.*)

    Because I choose to see life as challenging and dynamic, it is.

18. Belief: If there were no struggle, I might get bored.

    (Core Belief: *Life is painful.*)

    Because I choose to see life as challenging and dynamic, I can create as much excitement as I choose.

19. Belief: I will not do something unless I can do it perfectly.

    (Core Belief: *I am not OK unless I am perfect.*)

    Because I know that what I do is not who I am, I can be satisfied and enjoy my best effort.

20. Belief: If I do something less than perfect, I feel upset.

    (Core Belief: *I am not OK unless I am perfect.*)

    Because I know that what I do is not who I am, I can relax and enjoy my best effort.

21. Belief: If I get close to someone, I might lose myself.

    (Core Belief: *It is too risky to be vulnerable.*)

    Because I have the power to take care of myself when I am vulnerable, I am safe.

22. Belief: If I let myself get close to someone, they might leave me and I could not survive the hurt.

    (Core Belief: *It is too risky to be vulnerable.*)

    Because I have the power to take care of myself when I am vulnerable, I know it is safe to take risks.

By consciously choosing the information you want your brain to act on, you assume control over your life. No backseat driving for you!

Long ago Buddha was asked, "Are you a God?"
Buddha replied, "No."
"Are you an angel?"
He again replied, "No."
"What are you?"
And Buddha replied, "I am awake."

Five

OVERCOMING YOUR LIMITATIONS

IN the last chapter, we showed how you can take control of your life by transcending your *counter-connection*. But can Conscious Connection enable us to determine our futures?

In this chapter, we describe how mental conditioning—the Exercise of Conscious Connection—allows you to play the lead role in shaping your future. The more aware you are of what is happening inside yourself, the more you can make use of your enormous capabilities. The more connected you become, the more clarity and strength you have for resolving your problems, even the most dire and difficult situations. When you are connected, you are AWAKE.

Over the years, we have counseled hundreds of clients in Conscious Connection. In case after case, we find that our clients must confront what they think are their limitations if they are to succeed in achieving their goals. They had formed mental barriers that actually determined their abilities. Success was only possible once these limits were removed. We recall the words of one client, Jill L., shortly after her final therapy session, "I know now that the only limits to my potential are those I set myself."

The following account of a scientific experiment illustrates how Jill's realization has been demonstrated by a Russian researcher, Vladimir Raikov[1]. In 1976, Raikov hypnotized a group of students and told them they were historical figures possessing extraordinary talent in their field of study. Art students were told that they were Rembrandt, music students that they were Chopin. Raikov then asked the students to imagine themselves performing as Rembrandt or Chopin. A control group of students was asked to do the same thing, but not under hypnosis. The results were dramatically different. The hypnotized students performed far better than the control group, even though the latter had done the same imaginative role-playing. The hypnosis, in bypassing the conscious mind which often sets limits on our capabilities, allowed for the emergence of hidden talents.

---

1 Krippner, Stanley. "'Set' Psychology and Human Potentials." in *Journal of Humanistic Psychology*. Fall 1986, Vol. 26, No. 4.

Like hypnosis, Conscious Connection is a way of focusing your attention in a specific direction. This concentration of mental power allows you to ignore all distractions, creating an opening for new thoughts and feelings. Think of connecting as a form of self-hypnosis. By implanting your Conscious Connection in your mind, you can create any feeling or state of being you choose.

Training your mind is infinitely easier when you no longer hold the belief that limits you. In fact, the human mind is limited only by the way we think about it. A good example is how we allow Intelligence Quotient (IQ) Tests to define our "intelligence." As soon as people know their score on an IQ test, they tend to place boundaries around themselves. In other words, when people believe they are dumb—whether because of a test result, the treatment of a parent, or negative reinforcement in school—they frequently "live up" to that low expectation. Rather than achieve to the best of their abilities, they give in to feelings of inadequacy and failure. If such negative feelings control your mind, it is impossible to perform at your full potential.

Past experiences often determine how far we believe we can go. If we decide to learn a new language for example, we assume, based on our own and other people's experiences, that it will take a certain period of study. If our prior efforts at mastering a language have been laborious, that mindset influences our present and future endeavors. Free of such encumbrances, our capacity exceeds all expectations.

Sherry remembers being amazed when her college friend Sandy learned the basics of Greek in one day. Sandy didn't consider this as an astonishing feat, but merely the natural result of her focused concentration and desire. She believed there was no limit to how quickly she could learn.

The concept of limitlessness is exciting, but it can also be frightening. We generally feel more in control, and therefore safer, when there are explanations for everything—from how we think the way we do, to how we came to be the way we are. Our need for secure definitions creates absolutes and boundaries that are often not aligned with objective truth. Clearly, accepting the concept of limitlessness is antithetical to this need. But what would happen if the need were to suddenly disappear? Try this:

Close your eyes and take a few minutes to consider your thoughts and feelings about the limits you set for yourself.

Recall a specific time within the last year that you imposed a limitation on yourself.

Imagine what would have happened in that situation if you were free of the limit.

If you find the prospect of limitlessness awesome, you are not alone. It is a universal feeling. Although releasing the restrictions you place on yourself may feel like an insurmountable hurdle, don't be discouraged; when you set your mind to it, you can do it. Furthermore, we have discovered that the benefits of Conscious Connection do not stop with you. If you live your life to the fullest, you will influence the lives of others.

The potential of Conscious Connection for transforming our society begins with individuals. Imagine the results if a concentrated group of people focused on Conscious Connection. You come in contact with many people each day—at the gas station, the office, the grocery store, on the telephone . . . . What would happen if you behaved in a way that reflects your Conscious Connection? Quite possibly the experience of centeredness could be transmitted through space and time, setting off a chain reaction that reverberates throughout our society. How might this effect our ability to live harmoniously and lovingly?

Thomas S. Kuhn, History of Science Professor at M.I.T., studied how change occurs in science. He observed that, in every age, certain scientific views, structures, or paradigms prevail. When new ideas emerge that are inconsistent with established views, scientists strongly resist changing their minds. For example, the Heimlich Maneuver, used to clear the air passage when an individual is choking, was not officially accepted by the Red Cross until twelve years after it's discovery. Today, it is reputed to save more than four thousand lives per year worldwide. Nevertheless, ideas as dramatically new as Einstein's, Galileo's, or Darwin's create a changing reality so provocative, exciting and stimulating, that it becomes difficult to remain entrenched in old paradigms. Scientists are compelled to explore these new approaches.[2]

Applying Kuhn's theory of change to society and indi-

---

2 "Scientific Theories Suggest a Light at the End of the Tunnel." *The Tarrytown Letter*, March, 1982.

viduals illustrates how difficult it can be to relinquish old ideas, rituals, and beliefs in favor of new ones. Even in the face of overwhelming evidence that old ideas are no longer functional, we cling to the familiar. To change requires that we believe in our capacity to determine our experience— our very reality—by changing our personal thinking paradigms. Whatever you consider a barrier, you must confront and destroy. You can only win this battle when you approach your barriers from a different perspective. For example, if you are afraid of standing up and speaking in front of a large group of people, participating in a conference might be perceived as an exciting opportunity to confront your fear. If attending a social event alone is difficult, forcing yourself to spend a few hours at a party could be considered a challenge, a time to garner your inner capacities and strengths. This kind of shift in thinking is the quantum leap which will allow you to move to a higher level of growth and self expression. As scientists unlock their capabilities, they may find a way of explaining the mystery of how the mind and brain function. Until then, don't let the failure to understand a new idea interfere with the unfolding of your potential.

Perhaps you think only exceptional people are capable of exceptional acts. After learning about an outstanding achievement, you might find yourself thinking, "Wow! That's incredible! How can she do that? I could never do it!" Within those statements reside the self-imposed limits that prevent you from expressing your own remarkable gifts. The exercise of **Conscious Connection** aligns you with your true nature, allowing you to move beyond whatever you have previously believed to be your limitations. Because you have not yet experienced the boundlessness of your potential, you believe that all sorts of achievements are impossible. Once Conscious Connection frees you, you will break through your limiting barriers. The impossible will become commonplace. This can happen in a flash, as it did when Mozart heard an entire symphony in his head, or when the theory of relativity came to Einstein in a dream. You may not be able to duplicate a Mozart or Einstein, but you can certainly push beyond your personal self-limiting beliefs. Basic to both kinds of breakthroughs is your willingness to quiet your conscious mind so that your creative impulses naturally emerge. As you read the following examples, think about how you might consciously choose to embrace and activate your unique potential.

Stephen Hawking of Cambridge University overcame seemingly insurmountable obstacles to become perhaps the most brilliant theoretical physicist since Einstein. Hawking has Lou Gehrig's disease, which prohibits all normal speech and bodily movements. Confined to a wheelchair, he communicates through a computer apparatus that he operates with one finger, typing at a rate of only ten words per minute. Despite his physical and emotional challenges, Hawking has expressed some of our most important, creative and exciting ideas about the universe.

Christopher Nolan is not quite thirty and lives in Dublin, Ireland. He was born with brain damage that left him unable to speak or use his limbs. Today he is a prize-winning author. After winning his first award for a book of poems he wrote as a teenager, he went on to capture Britain's highest literary acknowledgement, the Whitbread Book of the Year Award in 1988. Nolan didn't begin writing until 1977, when a therapist discovered that through the use of a muscle-relaxing drug he could control his neck enough to type. A pointer was attached to his forehead, and Nolan could make contact with the typewriter by nodding his head. It sometimes takes him ten minutes to type just one word.

Contemplate for a moment how you feel after reading about these successful individuals. Helpless? Overwhelmed? Sad? Scared? Do you know where these feelings are coming from? Their source is the part of you that believes in limitations and thinks there is no other way to feel. Had the people in our examples been consumed by such emotions, they would never have been able to engage in life the way they do. Instead, they discovered the indestructible source within themselves—the place of Conscious Connection. They exemplify the human capacity to transcend physical and emotional limitations that might otherwise result in immobilization.

We could cite countless similar instances in the world of sports. Remember how the myth of the four-minute mile exploded in 1954? Contrary to unanimously supported scientific "fact" that it was physically impossible to beat that time, Roger Bannister did it, as did forty-seven others within the next two years. To date, twenty-four hundred people have accomplished what was absolutely believed to be impossible. One runner, Steve Scott, has broken the four-minute mile one hundred times. How can this be explained? Very simply. Roger Bannister was not aware of the prevailing belief. He was too busy training to read the scientific journals. He believed breaking the four-minute mile was possible. Bannister's belief enabled him to realize his goal.

While mass belief systems set external limitations on our thinking, other limitations are self-imposed. For example, Val Alekseyev, a world class weight lifter, believed he had reached his limit when he repeatedly lifted 499.9 pounds. Each time he attempted 500 pounds, he failed. Intuiting that Alekseyev was holding himself back and negating his true abilities, his trainer adjusted the weight without telling him. Alekseyev thought he was lifting the old weight. He successfully lifted 501.5 pounds.[3]

Sherry's eight and a half month old granddaughter, Nicole, needed no such ploy to climb stairs for the first time. One day, Nicole crawled over to the staircase and eyed it excitedly, clearly with some intent in mind. She put one hand on the second stair and one knee on the first. Then, seemingly by accident, she put the other knee on the bottom stair, and looked around with pleasure. Within seconds, she was off to the top of the staircase, never hesitating, never looking back, never doubting her ability, and obviously delighted with herself. Because her mind was unfettered with limiting beliefs, she could use her capabili-

---

3 Pulos, Lee, "Visions of the Future Mind." Dreaming the New Dream Conference. San Francisco, California. Fall, 1988.

ties to the fullest and reap the resultant joy.

How many times, and in how many ways have you limited yourself? Take a moment to examine how you throttle your experience of life by your perception of personal, physical, mental and emotional limitations. These are easy to spot because they usually begin with I CAN'T, or I AM NOT. For example:

> I can't have a fulfilling relationship.
>
> I didn't have a normal childhood so I can't ...
>
> I can't get along with my boss ... or my mother-in-law ... or
>
> I am not smart enough ...
>
> I have only average intelligence so I can't ...
>
> I am not a natural athlete so I can't ...

In your notebook, write down *your* I CAN'TS AND I AM NOTS.

Take heart. We are only dealing with beliefs. As we discovered in chapters Three and Four, beliefs are nothing more than habitual thought patterns, and they can be changed. The ideas presented in this chapter verify that the power resides in each of us to control and determine our own reality. All we need do is accept the existence of our authentic self, connect to it, and our natural abilities emerge.

Science teaches that we must see in order to believe, but we must also believe in order to see. We must be receptive to possibilities that science has not yet grasped, or we will miss them.

BERNIE SIEGEL, M.D.

Six

THE MIND AS HEALER

AS we learn more and more through brain research, it becomes harder to deny the powerful tie between mind and body. Traditional medicine sees disease as a separate entity emanating from external sources, puts a label on it, and then treats it primarily with drugs and surgery. The field of Holistic Medicine views pain and disease as reflections of internal and/or external disharmony and conflict. It seeks to cure through understanding the interaction of the mind, body and environment. Wouldn't it make more sense to avoid using invasive procedures whenever possible by examining these connections? If we are to benefit from our own mental ability to heal, we need to change our perspective towards treating pain and disease. In this chapter, you will learn about the mind's amazing natural capacity to act as "healer." When the proper mental connection between mind and body is established, the possibilities for healing are astounding.

The functioning of the Multiple Personality—medically defined as "The presence of two or more distinct identities or personality states (each with its own relatively enduring pattern of perceiving, relating to, and thinking about the environment and self)."[1]— demonstrates our extraordinary mental powers. Lee Pulos, a Canadian psychologist who has done extensive research with multiples, tells us that people with this condition develop advanced parallel processing skills that allow them to access more than the ten to twenty percent brain capacity most of us utilize. His case histories show that multiples alter their physiological makeup as rapidly and completely as they do their mental and emotional states. Within two seconds they change the color of their eyes, their visual ability, blood pressure, heart rate and right/left hand dominance. As one personality, they can swim, play the piano, or speak a foreign language; as another personality they cannot. Pulos documented a case in which one personality had a third degree burn. In a span of several minutes, as another personality emerged, the burned area healed completely. When the first personality returned, the burn reappeared.

The multiples in the study were not only able to modify

---

1 American Psychiatric Association: *Diagnostic and Statistical Manual of Mental Disorders,* Fourth Edition. Washington D.C., American Psychiatric Association, 1994. p. 230.

the workings of their autonomic nervous systems, but also to affect their genetics, as in changing eye color. This occurred spontaneously and with no apparent effort! Multiples develop such abilities unconsciously as a means of coping with early trauma. But why couldn't the rest of us develop them by choice?

Research has shown that we can control bodily functions such as heart rate, blood pressure, endocrine and immune systems, and hormones. To effect a specific bodily function, we need to clearly focus our awareness and energy on that area. There are various passive and active methods of accomplishing this: transformational coping, biofeedback, hypnosis, imagery or visualization and meditation.

* *Transformational Coping,* (developed by
    S. C. Kobasa and S. R. Maddi[2]), involves the
    process of thinking optimistically about a
    stressful event, and taking action that puts
    you in charge of that event.

* *Biofeedback* trains you to control your
    involuntary functions such as heart rate
    and blood pressure through the use of
    electronic devices.

* *Hypnosis* is a form of deep relaxation that
    induces a trance state. While in trance,
    suggestions are planted in the unconscious

2 Justice, Blair. "Those who stay healthy." in *Noetic Sciences Review,*
    Summer, 1988. The Institute of Noetic Sciences. Sausalito,
    California. p. 9.

that will continue to control specific bodily, emotional or mental functions when not in trance.

* *Imagery or Visualization* entails focusing on a picture or an experience that epitomizes and brings about the desired change.

* *In Meditation,* you induce a relaxed state by focusing on the rhythm of your breathing, a visual image, or the mental repetition of a word or sound. This state alters your metabolism, balances and energizes all the bodily systems, and influences specific changes you want to occur through putting you in touch with your inner self.

By interpreting situations negatively, or by needing to control and impress people, we actually reduce the production of important antibodies that protect us from infection.[3] When our perceptions of the world are negative, we create a state of *dis-ease*, disharmony or discomfort in our bodies, that lowers our immunity. Our cardiovascular systems are similarly affected by our view of life and how we have learned and now choose to react to stress. Research has shown that if you are cynical, suppress your anger, or have a hostile attitude, your chances of having a heart attack, arteriosclerosis, or blocked arteries, are considerably increased.

---

3 Justice, Blair. "Those Who Stay Healthy," in *Noetic Sciences Review*, Summer, 1988. The Institute of Noetic Sciences. Sausalito, California. p. 10.

Our emotions influence the release of the neurotransmitter norepinephrine, which in large amounts may damage the lining of coronary arteries, injure the heart, and raise blood pressure. Clearly, beliefs, expectations and changes in our perceptions and experiences affect self-healing. Although we do not always know why this is true, innumerable examples from contemporary medicine demonstrate the powerful influence of the mind over the body.

In a set of experiments described by psychiatrist Jerome Frank[4] on the placebo effect, a group of patients was given either morphine, a placebo, or a mild pain-killer. When doctors thought that they were administering morphine, the placebo was twice as effective as when they thought they were giving a mild analgesic. Even when scientific methodology has difficulty explaining this kind of phenomena, we need to remain receptive.

The Simonton approach[5] teaches people with cancer to develop and use their "active imagination" to engage their immune system in killing the malignant cells. On a psychological level, the approach insists that each individual discover and understand what factors contributed to the breakdown of the immune system. Then, through learning skills such as meditation and visualization, patients are encouraged to enlist their "active imagination" to overcome

4 Ferguson, Marilyn. *The Aquarian Conspiracy: Personal and Social Transformation in the 1980's.* Jeremy P. Tarcher, Inc. Los Angeles, California, 1980. p. 249.

5 Kirsch, Jonathan. "Can Your Mind Cure Cancer?" in *New West*, January, 1977. p. 40.

their disease. Children with cancer, for instance, often picture their white blood cells as a fighting army that seeks out and destroys the diseased cells. Although the Simonton approach requires learning a positive attitude, relaxation, meditation, and visualization, it does not eschew traditional methods such as radiation. Rather, it works in tandem with those treatments.

In his book, *Love, Medicine and Miracles*, Dr. Bernie Siegel relates his experiences and conclusions about "exceptional patients" who healed themselves of cancer. He is convinced, by his own findings and by the scientific research of other doctors, "that the state of the mind changes the state of the body by working through the central nervous system, the endocrine system, and the immune system."[6]

As a result of orthopedic surgeon Robert Becker's[7] study of the body's electrical systems, electricity is now used to heal difficult cases of broken bones. Becker discovered that under hypnotic suggestion, patients could produce electrical changes in any part of their body to promote their own healing. This kind of research provides a scientific explanation for otherwise inexplicable cures induced by hypnosis, the placebo effect, and other non-traditional methods. Such case studies illustrate the extent to which each of us can actively participate in our own healing.

What do we know about the complex relationship between body and mind? The immune system is directly

---

6   Siegal, Bernie S. *Love, Medicine & Miracles*. Harper & Row, Publishers. New York, New York, 1986. p. 3.

7   Ibid., p. 69.

influenced by hormones, which in turn are influenced by stress reactions and nerve impulses from the brain.[8] The area of our brains responsible for regulating most of our body's autonomic life support systems, such as breathing, temperature, blood pressure and heartbeat, is the hypothalamus. The hypothalamus affects both the thymus and spleen, which are in charge of manufacturing the white blood cells that protect us from disease.

Think of the hypothalamus as a communication center that receives and sends messages. It connects with other regions of the brain via nerve fibers that control our emotions and thoughts. An example of a syndrome called "psychosocial dwarfism" given by Dr. Bernie Siegel in his book *Love, Medicine and Miracles* brings home the impact of this connection. If a child is living in an unhealthy atmosphere of hostility, and interprets it as a rejection, the child's emotional as well as physical growth can be literally stunted. The limbic system (the brain's emotional center) picks up on the interjected feelings of low self-esteem and sends a message to the hypothalamus to shut off production of growth hormones produced by the pituitary gland. The pituitary gland in charge of physical growth just stops working.[9]

On the molecular level, the DNA repair system is another protective agent that can be compromised by the

---

8 Justice, Blair. "Those Who Stay Healthy," in *Noetic Sciences Review*, Summer, 1988. Institute of Noetic Sciences. Sausalito, California. p. 10.

9 Siegel, Bernie S. *Love Medicine & Miracles*. Harper & Row, Publishers. New York, New York, 1986. p. 67.

way we deal with life. Researchers at Ohio State University have shown that the level of distress we experience directly influences the effectiveness of our DNA repair systems.[10] Even though we are exposed to chemicals and radiation in our food, water and environment, our DNA repair systems can protect us against the development of mutations and tumors. But what about the emotional toxins that we introduce into the mind/body environment? Attacking the emotional toxins that result from negative beliefs, such as self-loathing and helplessness, is as important as destroying pollutants in the natural environment.

There is no question that we as human beings possess the power to hurt and to heal our bodies. Replacing *counter-connection* with Conscious Connection insures a healthier physical body. By consciously connecting, we develop a vibrant and hopeful way of viewing the world. It is our most all-encompassing health insurance policy.

10 Justice, Blair. "Those Who Stay Healthy." in *Noetic Sciences Review*, Summer, 1988. The Institute of Noetic Sciences. Sausalito, California. p. 11.

Spirit is the light of the soul. Spirit is universal. Spirit is the creative energy of the Cosmos. The soul of man is not conscious of its powers until it is enlightened by Spirit. Therefore, to evolve and grow, man must learn to develop his own soul forces. All great creative geniuses do this, although some of them do not seem to be as conscious of the process as others.

JOHANNES BRAHMS

Seven

INVOKING THE MUSE

BECAUSE we are born connected to our true selves, we all begin life with great creative potential. Over time, however, we become separated from the sacred center of our beings. Most of us learn to distrust our thoughts and feelings because we feel pressured into conforming to parental and societal values; we consequently form beliefs about the world that are inconsistent with our true selves. In effect, we hide from ourselves, burying our unique human characteristics along with our potential. How can we return to our center, live from the inside out, and unleash our potential once this alienation has occurred? This chapter will guide you, step by step, along the path towards reunion with your authentic self.

In his 1926 book, *The Art of Thought*, British writer Graham Wallas provides a useful definition of the creative process.[1] According to Wallas, creative production occurs in four stages: preparation, incubation, illumination and verification.

In the **PREPARATION** stage, you need to clarify and fully identify the question, challenge, or problem to be solved. This is not just an academic exercise; your determination to discover the solution must be accompanied by an ardent desire for success. Exercising your strong intention and desire is the catalyst that frees your inherent creativity. You must immerse yourself in the subject, ferreting out every detail pertaining to it, and noting all possible solutions.

Once your preparation is complete, you move into the **INCUBATION** stage. Relax your cognition. Allow the work you have done to gel. Most of us have a tendency to repeatedly re-examine information and possible options in the hope of finding the right answer. This time-consuming process not only wastes energy, but also obstructs the unconscious working out of a solution. Your powerful creative resources only take over once you've turned off your conscious thoughts. Wallas suggests that meditation, daydreaming, relaxation exercises and even sleep foster unconscious problem-solving abilities because such activities focus the attention in one direction, allowing us to

---

1 Harman, Willis and Rheingold, Howard. *Higher Creativity: Liberating the Unconscious for Breakthrough Insights.* Jeremy P. Tarcher, Inc., Los Angeles, California. 1984. p. 21-49.

ignore everything else. This undisturbed concentration quiets the conscious mind. Our internal forces of inspiration are free to act.

The stage is now set for breakthroughs to occur in the **ILLUMINATION** mode. In this state of heightened awareness and expanded knowledge, solutions come in the form of ideas, images, or innovations. Although the results of these "flashes" are evident in every area of our lives, their creation remains a mystery.

In the case of spontaneous "illuminations" that seem to burst out of nowhere, a process of "preparation" and "incubation" might be occurring out of your awareness. These "illuminations" tend to come to light when the thinking/analyzing part of the brain is quiet. During such moments—while we are taking a walk, driving a car, or listening to music, for example—our unconscious creative powers can be hard at work. As we have discussed in previous chapters, traditional scientific methodology still frequently discounts the significance of discoveries born of illumination. How often do you discount images or ideas that seem to appear out of nowhere, assuming they are unworkable, unimportant, unreliable or "crazy?" Does needing evidence or proof of the viability of your ideas get in the way of your following them? What do you think might happen if you trusted and pursued your "flashes?" The next time you are suddenly inspired, try writing down your ideas. If you don't keep track of these fleeting thoughts, you will lose them forever.

In the final stage, **VERIFICATION**, "illumination" is experienced, worked with, and examined in the context of everyday reality, so that wishful thinking can be separated from true inner knowledge. One way to distinguish between the two is to go inward and pay attention to how you feel when your "illumination" rises to consciousness. When engaged in wishful thinking, our clients often describe feelings of internal discordance, as if something is not quite right inside. True inner knowledge leaves us feeling calm, harmonious and confident—the same kind of feeling experienced when we are Consciously Connected.

The workings of genius offer invaluable insights into the creative process. We were inspired by a series of intimate conversations between journalist Arthur Abell and Johannes Brahms, recorded before the great composer's death in 1897. The creator of some of the most inspired music of all time, Brahms did not consider his masterpieces to be accidental. Rather, they resulted from much study, constant practice, and his own unique way of going inward, which he referred to as "invoking the muse." Brahms is explicit in expressing how he connected with his creative forces; he made contact with his "soul-powers" by sitting in a quiet place with no distractions. In this way, Brahms created an altered state of consciousness, leaving his conscious mind temporarily in abeyance, and causing inspiration to flow from the depths of his being in full and elegant form.

Brahms was influenced by Lao Tsu, the great Chinese philosopher and founder of Taoism, who wrote, "We cannot define Spirit, but we can appropriate it."[2] The composer firmly believed that spiritual power could be accessed by any person who chose to do so, even if that power could not be clearly defined. The key is to have the conviction that it exists and the desire to experience it.

Brahms described vibrations running through his body that would "...assume the forms of distinct mental images." He said, "after I have formulated my desire and resolve in regard to what I want—namely, to be inspired so that I can compose something that will uplift and benefit humanity— something of permanent value happens."[3] Brahms' vibrations came with such force and speed that, unless he immediately wrote them down, they faded away.

Everyone has "illuminations." Revelations flow naturally from the minds of children until they are stifled by adults, who through their desire to be socially correct, discard them as childish fancy. One of the great tragedies of Western civilization is that it has imbued in most of us the notion that someone else always knows best. Instead of learning to trust our inner selves, we designate parents, educators, clergy, physicians, and a host of other "experts" as the authorities.

If you doubt the validity of your illuminations, you ignore or discard many valuable insights. When you re-contact your inner self, trust in its reliability and value, then implement the four components of the creative process, you

---

2 Abell, Arthur M. *Talks with Great Composers.* Philosophical Library. New York, 1877. p. 13.

3 Ibid., p. 15.

will release your own creative forces.

Live Inside Out Not ▪ *Upside Down* was birthed in just this way. In 1986, we (Sherry and Fran) were working with an educational organization, Beyond War. The purpose of the group was to instill the concept that everything on the planet is interconnected, teach individuals to resolve conflict non-violently and learn how not to pose an enemy. These concepts had tremendous impact on our individual lives. We particularly struggled with the reality of not posing an enemy and found it was extremely difficult to put into everyday living. It meant fundamental changes in the way we thought about ourselves and others. It required giving up judgement, being right, blaming and seeing ourselves as victims. Most often this was a tedious process involving endless discussion and analyzation. In order for us and others to be willing to do this on a consistent basis, a way had to be found to make this process simpler, more immediate and lasting. We knew this change in thinking was valuable because when successful, we felt empowered, accepting, and peaceful and knew we were in contact with the best part of ourselves.

The challenge became how to communicate and teach these ideas not only to our individual clients but to as many people as possible. We immersed ourselves in observing and studying how people change their thinking. Determined to discover the best way to do this, we researched hypnosis, imagery, religion and prayer, philosophy, meditation, physics and psychological constructs (preparation phase).

Maintaining our commitment but refraining from

further analyzing and rehashing, we believed the answer would come (incubation phase).

The idea came to us that if we started with contacting the best part of ourselves first, then our perspective and perceptions of troubling situations would be transformed. The exercise, we later called Conscious Connection, quickly evolved (illumination phase).

We started to use the exercise personally and with our clients to see how effective it was in centering us and shifting our perspective and energy. It worked extremely well. Although it went through a series of refinements over time, it was exactly the process we were looking for, one that was easy and effective. After examining it, we realized it included many of the components that we knew to be relevant through our research and experience (verification phase).

Try this four step process now or whenever you have the desire to create.

Find a quiet place free of distractions, get consciously connected, and like Brahms, invoke the muse within you.

Notice how in the preparation phase, you can easily and clearly identify the problem to be solved.

In the incubation stage, observe how, when you are consciously connected, your penchant to continuously re-analyze is over shadowed by your calm.

In the illumination stage, pay attention to how, when you are consciously connected, your "flashes" come through freely.

Maintain your connection through the verification stage.

In the verification stage, when Consciously Connected, your ability to distinguish between true illumination and wishful thinking is immediate.

Intelligence highly awakened is intuition,
which is the only true guide in life.

KRISHNAMURTI

Eight

BELIEVING IN YOURSELF

IF human beings could land on the moon in spite of the vast unknown hurdles, surely we can explore the boundless regions of our own hearts and souls. We are inherently equipped with all we need to attain our special form of greatness. Practicing the exercise of Conscious Connection enables us to focus inward and let our special truths emerge.

We have previously discussed how the scientific community and Western society distrust what is not concrete and measurable, even in the face of opposing evidence. In their book *Higher Creativity*, Willis Harman, president of the Institute of Noetic Sciences, and Howard Rheingold, human behavior columnist for *Esquire*, refer to breakthrough experiences of Descartes and Mozart in relation to this phenomenon:

> Surprisingly, in the case histories of scientists, we found not only many specific scientific discoveries but the very foundations of science itself were built on breakthrough experiences, later backed up by empirical investigation. It is ironic that science, the institution that has most strongly branded these kinds of experiences as daydreams, delusions, or hallucinations, appears to have been born in just such a state—in a fever dream, in a flash to an individual who could not solve the problem with the conscious portion of the mind.[1]

Family environments often feed into this constraining framework by discouraging children from using inner abilities. Because of our obsession with conformity and the desire for predictability, we too often insist that children fit prescribed modes of thinking, being, feeling and behaving. Our educational system similarly ignores our inner capacities by maintaining the supreme importance of rational analysis. These societal forces cause our children to become incomplete and constricted human beings. In order to break free of these constraints, we need to let go of our limiting assumptions. We must examine our fears, open to new dimensions, and accept a broader definition of intelligence

---

1   Harman, Willis and Rheingold, Howard. *Higher Creativity: Liberating the Unconscious for Breakthrough Insights.* Jeremy P. Tarcher, Inc., Los Angeles, California. 1984. p. 5-6.

to include creativity and intuition, as well as rational analysis.

According to *Webster's New World Dictionary*, intuition is "the direct knowing or learning of something without the conscious use of reasoning, immediate apprehension or understanding."[2] Intuition is free from analytical thinking, fear, beliefs, opinions and conclusions. It is inner listening of the highest form. When we use and trust our inner voices, we experience a profound sense of peace and strength. We are Consciously Connected.

At first, it may seem illogical to follow your intuition. We are trained to ridicule those who act on "a whim" or obey "a voice inside." The term "feminine intuition" is frequently used in a negative way to describe an illogical or emotional response to life. However paradoxical it may seem, intuitive knowledge is the most logical source of information because it is true knowing. Intuition is a direct line to the center of your being; free of distortions, filters or interference, it is the place of Conscious Connection. When you venture deep inside yourself and listen to your inner voice, you will call forth amazing results in the form of ideas, actions and creations. In the following example, you will see how Karl W., fifty-seven, a successful accountant who had been seeing Sherry for several months, resolved a major conflict by allowing his intuition to guide him.

2 Guralnik, David B., ed. in chief. *Webster's New World Dictionary of the American Language*, Second College Edition. Prentice Hall Press, Cleveland Ohio. 1984.

Though the financial compensation was excellent, Karl's career as an accountant had never been satisfying or challenging to him. No matter how hard he tried, he couldn't ignore his feelings. A nagging voice deep inside kept saying, "Something has to change." The louder the voice became, the more difficult it was for Karl to accept his present situation.

Karl was at a crossroads; he could either go on as he was and feel perennially dissatisfied, or listen to his inner promptings and make a change. When he allowed himself to listen, he heard himself saying, "Write. You always wanted to be a writer. Do it now!" As a young man in college, he had done a lot of creative writing and edited a university publication. Karl found writing exciting, stimulating and fulfilling. His intuition told him to follow his life-long yearning to be a writer.

Although Karl had lots of fears attached to starting something new and losing a dependable salary, when he consistently connected, and listened to his inner voice, he knew what he had to do. Karl decided to take the plunge. Immediately after making writing his career, Karl felt free and exuberant. He reduced the demands of his accounting practice by not taking any new clients, and put his energy into establishing his credentials as a writer. He knew that had he relied on rational thinking alone without his intuition, he would not have heard his inner voice and allowed himself to follow his dream.

Trusting your "inner knowing" is a process which, optimally, begins in early childhood. Self-trust needs to be encouraged and practiced. Did you get reinforced for paying attention to your thoughts and feelings? If the answer is yes, then trust in the importance of your inner promptings was established. If, on the other hand, you felt discouraged or ridiculed when you expressed some of your thoughts or feelings, the process of trusting yourself was blocked. Over time, self-doubt obscured the pathways to your inner being. Then you either became dependent on the outside environment to determine how you should think and feel, or distrustful of both your outer and inner world.

In order to follow your intuition, you must first acknowledge its existence. If you deny your "inner knowing," you will feel confused and anxious due to the conflict between what you know to be true and your denial of it. Unearthing the source of your self-doubt is the key to becoming free of it, as Sherry's client, Laura, discovered through the following dialogue:

LAURA: *My friend Sara proposed a business partnership this week. I don't know whether I should do it or not.*
SHERRY: *Do you want to do it?*
LAURA: *Yes, and no. I'm very interested in the work, but I don't know if I can trust Sara. She lies sometimes.*
SHERRY: *What does she lie about?*
LAURA: *Oh, not important things usually, except once. Last spring, I brought her into a catering business, and she cheated me out of some of my share of*

the profits.

SHERRY: *How did you feel when you found out?*

LAURA: *Well, I knew she needed the money badly herself ... I don't know how I felt ... I guess I didn't think about my feelings.*

SHERRY: *Did you ever suspect that she was cheating you before you knew for sure?*

LAURA: *Maybe I kind of knew ... but I wasn't really sure.*

SHERRY: *Do you often ignore your "hunches"?*

LAURA: *Yeah. I usually think I must be wrong.*

SHERRY: *And do you often not know how you feel in a situation?*

LAURA: *I guess so. I don't think about it much.*

SHERRY: *Do you remember a time when you were a little girl, and you had a strong feeling about something, but questioned if you were right to feel that way?*

LAURA: *Lots of times! When I would look at my Mom, she would look furious. Her face would be red. She'd squint her eyes and frown. I'd feel scared and ask her why she was angry.*

SHERRY: *Yes—and then what?*

LAURA: *She'd smile, a really tight smile, and say, "Oh, no dear, I'm not angry. Mommy doesn't get angry. You must be imagining it."*

SHERRY: *And how did you feel then?*

LAURA: *I'd get all confused and feel like I was imagining things.*

SHERRY: *So you learned to distrust your feelings and intuition as a youngster.*

LAURA: *I see . . . so that's why I'm never sure of what I am feeling, or if it's real.*

SHERRY: *Right. If you were to go inside yourself right now, get consciously connected and trust what you know to be true about going into business with Sara, what would the answer be?*

LAURA: *(After a short pause . . .) DON'T DO IT!*

SHERRY: *Good for you! Remember that your intuition is the very best guide you can have.*

You can see where you stand in this vital area of trusting your intuition by responding to the following statements:

TRUST QUESTIONNAIRE

IN YOUR NOTEBOOK, WRITE DOWN ANY STATEMENT THAT IS TRUE FOR YOU. BASE YOUR ANSWER ON WHAT IS TRUE MORE THAN 10% OF THE TIME.

1. I depend on recognition and approval from others to determine how I feel about myself.
2. I feel confused, unsure or worried about making decisions.
3. I allow others to make decisions for me.
4. I allow others to cancel out my decisions.
5. I consider my feelings unimportant.
6. My behavior is in conflict with my feelings.
7. I consider my thoughts unimportant.

8. My behavior is in conflict with my thoughts.

9. My feelings, thoughts, and behavior are in conflict with one another.

Now you have some idea of how much confidence you place on your intuitive processes. Ultimately, the goal is to answer FALSE to all the questions. You need to work on the areas to which you answered TRUE. When you practice the following affirmations, you provide your mind with alternatives. As the new beliefs become embedded, the old ones sink deeper into your mental files and lose their power over you. The more often you input the new data, the more quickly change will occur.

Input the affirmative statements with the same diligence that you practice Conscious Connection. Give yourself permission to remember to practice. When you forget, forgive yourself. Self-criticism is the *only* mistake to beware of. For now, practice incorporating the following affirmative statements into your being every time you consciously connect. Express your strong intention by practicing them frequently—once per hour is ideal.

AFFIRMATIVE STATEMENTS

---

1. I depend on my own recognition and approval to determine how I feel about myself.

2. I feel clear and calm when I make decisions.

3. I make my own decisions.

4. When I make a decision that is right for me, I adhere to it.

5. I consider my feelings important.

6. My behavior is in harmony with my feelings.

7. I consider my thoughts important.

8. My behavior is in harmony with my thoughts.

9. My feelings, thoughts, and behavior are in harmony.

When you trust what you know to be true for you, you can apply and maintain Conscious Connection in your life. Trusting your intuition is a major precondition for staying consciously connected. Your inner knowledge will guide you in every way, from making the simplest decision to embarking on the greatest personal challenge.

Just one person who listens to his or her inner voice can change the world. If you have the courage to act on what you "know" to be possible without requiring mounds of evidence, your action will encourage others to do the same. You will create a dynamic synergy that will lead to personal and societal transformation. Conscious Connection demands that you engage your true, intuitive self.

Think about the far-reaching impact of a man like Mahatma Ghandi. Clearly, Ghandi did not derive his power and conviction from external sources. In *Ghandi and the Good Life*,[3] writer Suman Khanna recalls an occasion when Ghandi addressed the English House of Commons for over two hours without any notes. Ghandi's ability to speak impromptu so long and eloquently baffled the London

3 Khanna, Suman. *Ghandi and the Good Life*. Ghandi Peace Foundation. New Delhi, India. 1985, p. 112.

reporters. When they asked his secretary for an explanation, she replied, "What Gandhi thinks, what he feels, what he says, and what he does are all the same. He does not need notes. You and I think one thing, feel another, say a third, and do a fourth, so we need notes and files to keep track." What better proof do we need that authenticity is an indomitable force?

Centuries ago, Aristotle said that the true nature of anything is the highest it can become. All of us are born with boundless capabilities in the realms of thinking, feeling, imagination, creativity, intuition, insight, talent, and foresight. All it takes is making the shift from doubting yourself to believing in your authentic self. You have the inner resources to make the leap!

Man ultimately decides for himself!
And in the end, education must be education
toward the ability to decide.

VIKTOR FRANKL

Nine

QUESTION YOUR PRIORITIES

HOW often have you made a decision that you thought was right for you, only to find that it didn't feel right after all? How many people do you know who invest years in studying a particular field, only to realize that they are unhappy doing their chosen work? Why does this happen? Because many of us have no idea what we truly value. We chase after approval and status, money and achievement, thinking that these things will bring us fulfillment. Even though such attributes may count among our values, after self-examination, we find that they are not nearly as important as qualities that bring us more personal satisfaction. The experience of Fran's friend, Jennifer, is not uncommon:

Jennifer graduated at the top of her class, and earns a

comfortable income from her job placement service. Despite her successes, Jennifer found herself feeling increasingly imprisoned by her business and consequently unhappy. Fran encouraged her to try the Conscious Connection process and then explore what was really important to her. Jennifer decided to take a few weeks off from work so she could devote all her energy to figuring things out for herself. The more she got in touch with her true self, the more Jennifer discovered that her priorities needed to be re-shuffled to reflect her personal value system.

She realized how important her love of nature and physical activity were to her. Once she adjusted her actions to reflect her value system, Jennifer found herself happier and more energetic. She hired an accountant to worry about the accounting details of her business, and spent that extra time taking a course in rock-climbing. Not surprisingly, Jennifer's employment service made its biggest profit ever.

What are values? Why do we need to know about them? Values are anything we consider to be desirable or worthy. They are standards that determine the ethics, mores, ideals and social principles of individuals and societies. They include such qualities as honesty, politeness, cleanliness, productivity, obedience, equality, sharing and cooperation. Values differ enormously from one country, religion, educational system and family to another. In King Arthur's court, the prevailing values of chivalry, honor and romance determined everyday behavior. The Puritan Fathers esteemed hard work, self-sacrifice and thrift. One religion may accentuate forgiveness, another stress "an eye for an eye." Some educational institutions underscore the achievement of high grades; others highlight the love of learning. Families emphasize a gamut of values—from love, closeness and commitment, to duty, competition and accomplishment. Imagine, for a moment, how different your values would be if you were born into the British royal family. What if you were the child of migrant farm workers? In each case, how much importance would you place on higher education? How crucial would financial security be?

Values not only differ *between* institutions, but change over time, within any one institution. In the nineteenth century for example, the United States made a historic shift in values by abolishing slavery and proclaiming the right of every human being to be free. Since values influence everything we do, say, think or feel, it is crucial to understand the values that compose your individual life view.

Think about the values that are significant to you right now. List them, using the following four-step formula. When you are connected to your true self, determine your true values and prioritize them, your behavior will become consistent with your life view. Achieving congruence between your ideals and actions represents a major leap towards maintaining Conscious Connection.

FORMULA FOR UNDERSTANDING VALUES

STEP ONE: IDENTIFICATION

The first task is to identify the values that guide your life now.

Divide a page in your notebook vertically into two sections. On the left side write the word VALUES on top, on the right hand side write the word ORIGIN. The following list of values gives some examples which may or may not apply to you. To get the most benefit from this exercise, take the time to add any values that are not on the list and any that you wish to strive towards in the future. Be sure to delete from the list any values that have no importance for you.

Examples

integrity	being loving
responsibility	health
forgiveness	beauty
intelligence	possessions
ambition	friendship
power	fun
excitement	privacy
independence	faith
sports	security
outwitting others	humor
notoriety	logic
courage	obedience
politeness	self-control
family	harmony

Now you have identified your values. Step Two will help you discover the underlying source of each one. Knowing where your values come from will give you a clearer picture of why you think, feel and act in certain ways.

STEP TWO: ORIGIN

It is impossible to form ideals in isolation from external influences.

Values emanate from a variety of sources including yourself, your parents and siblings, the culture, religion and social institutions into which you were born. Try the following exercise:

---

* Take each value from your list, one at a time, and think for a moment what would happen if you eliminated it. Would anyone disapprove, or be angry or disappointed with you? Would you be upset with yourself?

* In the right hand column of your worksheet, write who would feel strongly if you negated the value. It might be any or all of the following: another person, an institution, a culture or yourself. This is the origin of your present value.

* Think about what purpose the value serves or served for that person or institution.

* What was the context in which it originated for them?

For instance, one or both of your parents may value frugality because they were poor as children, and fear that the same misfortune could happen again. This makes them more cautious than present reality may dictate. You may have unconsciously adopted that value as yours, without recognizing how it developed and the difference in your circumstances.

As a child it's frightening to challenge the values you grow up with because you are dependent for your emotional and physical survival on the various systems that uphold these values. Once internalized, it is impossible to distinguish a value based on external sources from your own true values without engaging in this kind of examination.

As you think about your values and discover some that no longer resonate with you, you may feel scared at the prospect of giving them up. This is an old fear, left over from when you were dependent on others for survival. Now your situation has changed. The scared feeling will seem very real before you realize that it is based on the past. Once you uncover this unconscious process, you can move beyond your fear. You can clarify the values that are yours, choosing those you want to maintain and those you want to eliminate. Until you do this, you unwittingly allow an internal struggle that causes you to feel guilty and anxious. When you have organized your value system, you permit yourself to become whole, connected and autonomous.

STEP THREE: DISCRIMINATION

In establishing your true values, it is very important to be completely honest with yourself. This can be difficult because of what you THINK your values ought to be. Nevertheless, objectivity is essential. Placing either a good or bad connotation on a value can falsely influence whether or not you accept that value as yours. Giving a value a negative connotation might incline you to eliminate it from your list, as most of us do not want to be identified with something we regard as "bad." Conversely, a positive association may cause you to accept a value that really derives from outside sources.

Put all judgements aside. Examine each value objectively. Decide if you want to retain it or cross it off your list. Even if a value did not originate with you, you may still want to keep it.

---

* Draw a line through those values you intend to completely eliminate.

Establishing priorities provides a way of determining your best choice of action in every situation. Now that you have a list of twenty to thirty values, it is time to divide it into primary and secondary groups.

---

* Organize your values into two groups by going through your list and putting number 1 by those values that are primary in your life right now. Mark the remaining values with a number 2.

You may have to repeat this process a few times in order to arrive at a final list of ten to fifteen values numbered 1. This represents your PRIMARY GROUP. Your SECONDARY GROUP will contain the rest. When one value seemingly conflicts with another, prioritizing helps you make decisions in accordance with your life view.

Suppose, for example, that a new job offer requires you to make a decision. It presents advancement opportunities, but demands long hours. On your value list, time with your family is a primary consideration; status and money are secondary. Clearly, this would not be a good choice for you.

---

 * On the next page of your notebook, write LIFEVIEW at the top. Next divide the page in half horizontally and on the top half, write the words PRIMARY VALUES and on the bottom half, SECONDARY VALUES. Now, write your values in the appropriate sections.

 * Over time, the priority you place on specific values may change. Mark values that you would like to see become less important with zeros and those you want to become more important with stars.

By establishing which values are most important to you, you increase your self-knowledge. Now you are ready to act in alignment with your true self and to deal successfully with situations that previously left you feeling confused and unsure about how to proceed.

STEP FOUR: ACTION

We all encounter special circumstances in which, for one reason or another, it seems difficult to act in harmony with our overall life view. Fran's husband, Rex, shared the following experience with us:

Rex, an architect, designed and built a contemporary house for a client in a natural hillside setting. Several years later, a new owner redecorated the interiors, and gave a party to which Rex was invited. He was introduced to the interior designer who asked whether he thought her work complemented his design. The question made him uncomfortable because he strongly disliked what she had done, but did not want to hurt her feelings. She had replaced the natural materials he had chosen to go with the rustic site— unpainted wood, plaster and ceramic tile—with glitzy mirrored ceilings and high-gloss plastics. The result was jarringly inconsistent with his original intent.

Although Rex was clear about his opinion, his concern that he might hurt her feelings kept him from responding honestly. Instead, he equivocated, communicating tacit approval. Immediately, he felt upset with his response. He knew he was being dishonest. The problem was, he felt he could not maintain his personal integrity and offer empathy at the same time.

Determining the best course of action in any situation, even a delicate one, depends on following three simple guidelines.

---

* DECIDING WHICH VALUE OR VALUES ARE RELEVANT: When a situation arises in which you feel uncomfortable, confused or challenged, and do not immediately know what to do, begin by identifying the value or values that are meaningful in that particular instance. Establish whether they are of primary or secondary importance.

* POSTULATING RESULTS: Speculate on the outcome of acting on each value by playing the situation through in your imagination and observing what effect each value has upon it. Consider the other people involved and, most important, your feelings about yourself.

> * CHOOSING A SUITABLE VALUE OR VALUES: After examining
> the hypothetical result connected with each relevant value,
> select the one (or more) values that is most in harmony
> with your thoughts and feelings. You will instinctively know
> which value (or values) is right for you. Remember that
> intuition is a form of inner knowledge. Trust and pay
> attention to your inner self.

After going through this process, acting in alignment with your inner truth follows naturally. You will then have the satisfaction of behaving in accordance with who you really are.

When we walked through this exercise with Rex, he saw immediately how he could have handled the party situation differently. First, he would have identified his values of integrity and empathy. Second, he would have postulated the results of acting on one value, and then the other. Third, he would have seen that sacrificing honesty for kindness, or vice versa, would not have been consistent with his true self. Because the two values were equally meaningful to him, he needed to act in a way that would reflect them both.

Instead of being stuck unnecessarily in an either/or position, Rex realized he could have responded in the following way: "I can see that you are obviously talented, but I would have chosen materials more in keeping with my original concept." Rex had no way of knowing how his response would be received. He could not have control over this external factor. However, because his caring was communicated by his effort to sincerely validate her, and he gave his honest opinion, he would have come away feeling as if he had been true to himself.

Although we tend to think of values in absolute terms, real life situations are rarely black or white. They usually involve interactions between one value and others that are pertinent to the particular circumstance. Thus, how we put our values into practice makes all the difference. Flexibility and moderation evoke infinitely more satisfying results than rigidity and excess. Take the value of obedience, for example:

Suppose you are a parent who feels adamantly about obedience. You ask your child to take out the garbage, and your child doesn't do it. You try reasoning, but it does not work. Blinded by the all-consuming importance you place upon obedience, you see no other option but to resort to force. Oblivious to the larger picture, you stop at nothing to obtain obedience from your child.

If you value obedience to this extreme degree, are you prepared for the consequences? In our experience, force precipitates hatred, fear, violence and alienation. Your determination to achieve the desired response, at all costs, could negatively effect your relationship with your child.

Suppose, on the other hand, you are a parent with only moderate dedication to obedience. Your child refuses to take out the garbage. You place importance on his doing the chore, but—since obedience is not an all-consuming value in the situation—you are able to consider what the purpose of the task is, and what you need to do to accomplish that purpose.

You realize that your goal is to teach your child a sense

of responsibility. With that in mind, you engage him in a discussion about his participation in family chores. When obedience is not your only focus, other values you deem important, such as cooperation, mutual respect and responsibility come into play.

Every value, held in the extreme, results in the inability to entertain alternatives. Think about this in terms of values such as love, harmony and integrity, power or security. Imagine what would happen if our society took these values to the extreme. For example, would an excessive attachment to harmony preclude the conflict and confrontation necessary for growth?

Maintaining values in a reasonable way allows you to find creative solutions to your problems and maintain loving relationships. Flexibility promotes healthy living and the ability to communicate and cooperate with people. Rigidity leads to lives dominated by constriction, parochial thinking and limited options. You are not being disloyal to your value system when you consider it necessary to moderate your stance. For example:

Sherry's client Jack worked for a company that expected its employees to make their jobs their first priority in life. Jack was required to work long hours, nights and weekends. As a result, he found himself physically and mentally exhausted, suffering from a classic case of burnout. Company policy maintained that a leave of absence was acceptable only if backed up by a written recommendation from a physician stating that the time off was necessary for medical reasons. Jack was torn; he didn't have an injury or symptoms such as a temperature, the flu or an infection. As serious as the side effects of burnout can be, the condition is not considered quantifiable as a medical illness.

Faced with this dilemma, Jack got consciously connected and checked his value list. Integrity was a high priority. Taking care of himself was important too, but not to the same degree. In light of his conflicting values, Jack hesitated to ask his physician to stretch the truth in a medical recommendation, even though the time off was critical to his emotional and physical well-being. At first, he rigidly adhered to the value of integrity, unable to see how he might obtain the necessary rest. Sherry pointed out that being rigid about one value left no room for considering other values. In this case, a more flexible attitude towards his value would allow Jack to respect and meet his needs.

Jack discussed the problem with his doctor honestly, explaining the company rules, and together they came up with an acceptable plan. The doctor wrote a letter highlighting Jack's symptoms, alluding to their serious physical ramifications, and recommending a two-week rest. During his time off, Jack did some thinking and practiced consciously connecting. In the future, he decided to establish his own balance between work and personal life. He would adhere to what he thought was right for him, even if it meant leaving his present job. Jack now understood the necessity of examining each situation on its own merits, and acting in his best interests without guilt or conflict.

The following exercise gives you an opportunity to practice identifying some of your values. It will enable you to achieve results that reflect your inner truth.

Suppose a close friend of yours is in the hospital, desperately ill. Although death appears imminent, your friend is not ready to face that possibility. You go for a visit and she asks you imploringly if she looks better than she did the day before. In reality, she looks worse.

---

* What values are triggered as you think about how to respond?
* What would be the outcome of the actions associated with each value?
* Does one value take precedence over the other in this circumstance?
* How would you respond?

Use this process in every day life as a tool to make decisions and take actions that align with your true self. Even if using the FORMULA FOR UNDERSTANDING VALUES feels awkward and cumbersome at first, with practice it will become an automatic part of your thinking.

To stay connected to your own true nature you must trust your intuition, replace your negative programming with new beliefs, and establish your values. These are the foundation for remaining on solid ground with your authentic self.

NEW BELIEFS

CONSCIOUS CONNECTION

TRUST   VALUES

Because these three components are interconnected, when either beliefs, trust or values is out of balance, so are you. Conversely, corrections in one facilitate and reinforce change in the others.

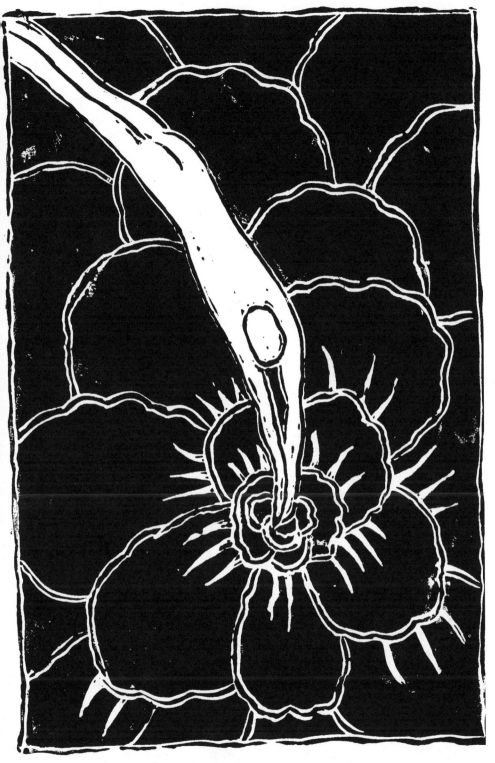

Delving into the center—finding one's essence

We can begin anywhere—everywhere.
Let there be transformation, and let it begin
with me.

Ten

LIVING YOUR TRUTH

IN *Think on These Things*, Krishnamurti sketches an evocative picture:

> I saw a boat going up the river at full sail, driven by the west wind. It was a large boat, laden with firewood for the town. The sun was setting, and this boat against the sky was astonishingly beautiful. The boatman was just guiding it, there was no effort, for the wind was doing all the work.[1]

This is a wonderful image to keep in mind. Sometimes we slog through life as though it were a swamp alive with

1 Krishnamurti, J. *Think on These Things*. Harper & Row, New York, 1964. p. 234.

crocodiles and quicksand. Yet, if we choose, we can sail through life on the winds of our Conscious Connection. The key is to feel our connection so deeply that we become one with our authentic self.

By now, you have probably discovered that having an occasional experience of connection is relatively easy—something like dieting or abstaining from alcohol or cigarettes for a day. Working to maintain your connection until it becomes part of you is a greater challenge. This effort requires an unshakable resolve that springs from a deep inner desire for self-determination which we all have, but sometimes block. Every time we tell ourselves that we are unworthy or incapable of making a commitment, unimportant, unlovable, and so on, we build inner barriers to our own connection.

The case of Jerry D., thirty-one, illustrates the kind of self-defeating patterns we can find ourselves trapped in. Jerry's connection is the experience of fulfillment. However, when he thinks he is unacceptable the way he is, Jerry immediately blocks his connection. One of the ways he reinforces his belief and feelings of insecurity is through dating. As soon as Marjorie indicated that she really appreciated him, Jerry immediately found a reason to end the relationship. He behaved in the same way with Anna and Constance, even though he really liked them both. Jerry simply cannot believe anyone could really love *him*.

Many of our clients believe that they are selfish if they take time and energy to focus on themselves. It all depends on how selfish is defined. We interpret selfish to mean focusing on oneself at the expense or exclusion of others. The activity we are describing, self-care, involves nurturing and loving oneself so that a state of well-being is experienced. This is what makes caring about others possible. Making the commitment to live inside out not upside down is synonymous with self-care. When you are consciously connected—in touch with your naturally giving self, you are incapable of acting in a selfish manner.

Engaging in the continuous process of consciously connecting is a special way of saying to yourself, "I love you." However, even when you decide to live from your authentic self, you are vulnerable to your old programming. Conscious Connection is an ongoing process that requires your constant awareness, vigilance and active involvement. Monitor your thinking, especially the subtle background noise that takes the form of criticism, judgement and admonishment. When you hear it, immediately ask yourself: "What is going on here? What are the facts?" Recognize that the old programming is speaking. Ask yourself, "How can I be loving to myself? What thoughts are consistent with being loving to me?" If you find you need help in doing this, don't hesitate to reach out for support. Talk to someone you know will understand, a friend, partner, or member of your family. Form a group with others who have decided to love themselves. Seek out a professional psychotherapist who is willing to work with you in this mode.

You've come a long way since you first experienced conscious connection in Chapter One. You have mastered the basics of reprogramming your negative beliefs, trusting

yourself, and determining the values that are really important to you. Now you are ready to experience Conscious
Connection in a more focused way. The words and images
you chose in Chapter One will trigger your Conscious
Connection. Used repeatedly, they will lock it into a new file
that your brain can access. Your brain is a file cabinet that
stores its files in the order of their importance. As you continually repeat your verbal and sensory images, your brain
moves your Connection file to the front. Now it is time to
re-experience Conscious Connection. Follow the exercise
that worked for you. Let it carry you to your Connected
state.

Sit back and close your eyes for a moment.

Take three deep breaths, and with each breath release any
tension you are holding.

Imagine the sun above your head shining its warm golden light
down upon you.

Allow every muscle in your body to relax as you feel this warm
light washing over you.

Imagine you have some magic dust.

Sprinkle it over yourself.

Know you have the power to reach the authentic you and to
feel truly centered.

You have felt this way before. If you need help recreating your
previous experience, allow the dust to spontaneously create this
feeling for you now.

Remember your trigger word that describes your conscious
connection and say it to yourself.

See yourself connected to your authentic self.

Focus in on your image.
    See the details . . .

Hear the sounds . . .
Savor any smells or fragrances . . .
Let yourself experience all the sensations that are a part of
your picture . . . as you connect to your authentic self.
Take a long moment and let this experience saturate your being.

As you open your eyes, continue to consciously experience
that image and feeling. Now, take three deep breaths and . . .

Close your eyes again. Imagine you have a movie camera.
Sharply focus in on your centering experience and all of
its details.
Run your movie in your mind now. This is what you will do
whenever you want to be centered.

Just as the musical score of a movie has the power to
change a scene from ominous to light-hearted, your connection is the determining background music of your life. It
will pervade everything you see and feel.

Once you have your file in place, acting on your connection is simple. See what happens when you re-experience
this exercise from Chapter One:

Pick a situation that is currently a thorn in your side, one that is
uncomfortable and unsettling. Take a deep breath and bring
your connection into your being by repeating the word, sensations and image you chose. Repeat them over and over again.
Pay no attention to anything else. Now play the thorny situation
through in your mind, using your connection as a backdrop for
that old, familiar scene. Within the new context of your connection, how will you behave? What outcome do you predict?

Of course, this works beautifully if you have the time to contemplate your actions before the situation blows out of proportion in the first place. It is easy to plan when you face an ongoing problem, in which you may interrupt the old scenario and change your actions at any point. But what do you do if you find yourself embroiled in an emotionally explosive situation? Does Conscious Connection work when you feel out of control and reason does not seem readily available? The answer is a resounding yes. You simply have to give yourself permission to think and feel at the same time. Even when it seems as if your emotions have total control over you, your reasoning powers are available and waiting in the wings for their cue to intercede. Call them on stage! You will be amazed at the tremendous power you possess. It doesn't matter at what point in the situation you switch gears and consciously connect. It is more important that you see you can connect and do it every chance you get. Eventually, you will be reprogrammed to instinctively think, feel and act in alignment with your Connection.

When you consciously connect, you announce to your whole being that you are in command of your every experience. If someone robs your house or cheats you in business, they are responsible for their actions and should be accountable for the consequences. But *you* are responsible for how *you* respond in every situation. You and you alone determine your responses to the external world. You can stay stuck in feeling depressed, angry or powerless, or you can choose to connect and allow yourself to move beyond

those feelings. As soon as you get into your conscious connection, you will find that staying depressed, angry, or powerless is not compatible with your connected state.
Choosing to connect is choosing to be in command of your
life, whether you have a thorny problem, an important
decision or a creative dilemma.

It is extraordinary how the same situation can be
handled very differently when you approach it from a different perspective. For example, let's say once again that you
have been robbed. You can do nothing to change the fact
you've been victimized, but you can take charge of your
present and your future. At first, you may have feelings of
sadness, loss and anger. But when you connect and engage
the best part of you, these feelings will no longer guide your
behavior. You will be able to think clearly and act in a way
that is consistent with your connected state. You will accept
your loss, take any action that will realistically prevent a
recurrence, and move on. When you act from your connection, the results are simply the natural outcome of your
taking control.

Become one with your connection by practicing it as
many times an hour as possible. Remember, the point is not
to struggle with your old program, but to embrace your new
one. Your old, negative habits simply slip away. It's like
cleaning a glass filled with dirty water. As you continually
pour in fresh water, the dirt is washed away. Because your
brain indiscriminately accepts whatever data you implant,
you must feed it positive information. Each time you
connect, your brain becomes a partner in making the expe-

rience of your chosen state an integral part of you. You have unearthed a buried treasure—your true nature. You will never be the same.

Epilogue

SURVIVAL OR CONSCIOUS EVOLUTION

As a human race, we have restricted our brains to the minimum functions necessary for survival. We have barely begun to tap our power. Our challenge if we are to determine the future of society and direct our own realities, is to utilize our enormous potential. In their book, *Higher Creativity*, Willis Harman and Howard Rheingold state that:

> In the alternative picture of evolution that is beginning to emerge from quantum physics we find that rather than consciousness evolving from the universe, the universe evolved from consciousness, and that consciousness seems to have 'pulled' the

evolutionary process in certain preferred directions, first in the direction of mind becoming aware of itself and then in the direction of becoming aware of its potentials. The implications of such a 'consciousness-produces-reality' conceptualization are so profound and far-reaching, not only for physics, but metaphysics, that one can easily imagine all institutions of society being profoundly affected.[1]

In other words, we have the ability to choose how we evolve. Either we continue in the direction of decay, and eventually self-destruct by misusing technology, or we embrace a higher consciousness, one of caring and cooperation, and use our technology in life-constructing ways.

Reaching the ultimate is a developing process. Each time we connect, we create a more evolved reality, one that is centered, loving and accepting. A reality where it would be possible to never hate another, do harm, act from fear, or be controlled by external negativity. Through the exercise of Conscious Connection—living inside out, we learn that as each one of us personally transforms, we have a greater impact on the direction of societal evolution than we ever dreamed. As a result of our actions, others will be inspired. Together, we can stretch this connected state to its limits.

When we are centered, we are an outstanding example for adults and children alike to emulate. As adults, we are the parents to all children, not just those we birthed. The

1   Harman, Willis and Rheingold, Howard. *Higher Creativity: Liberating the Unconscious for Breakthrough Insights.* Jeremy P. Tarcher, Inc. Los Angeles, California, 1984. p. 187.

planet is our responsibility and our children are the key to its future. Every child we come in contact with is irrefutably influenced by our presence and our actions, positive or negative. It follows that the responsibility to encourage a child's emotional growth rests with each and every one of us. The question is, how can we support and reinforce their natural authenticity?

We can begin by recognizing that children learn to trust and believe in themselves based on where they are in their emotional and mental development. By being sensitive to the individual child and talking on their own level, we can teach them how to Consciously Connect in ways they can grasp.

If we create a supportive environment, children will feel safe in exploring their boundaries, knowing that they will not be allowed to go beyond what they can handle. Children who are loved and accepted become loving, accepting adults, able to recognize that a troubled society is symptomatic of its members being off center, disconnected from their authentic selves. Therefore, it is important to carefully choose the adults we entrust the care of our children to, selecting them for their capacity to model loving, accepting behavior.

Consciously connected children become centered adults, and as this consciousness of mutuality, wisdom and love expands, it will produce a reality in which hunger, war, abuse, and violence cannot thrive.

Bibliography

Abell, Arthur M. *Talks with Great Composers.* Philosophical Library. New York, 1877.

American Psychiatric Association: *Diagnostic and Statistical Manual of Mental Disorders,* Fourth Edition. Washington D.C., American Psychiatric Association, 1994.

Ferguson, Marilyn. *The Aquarian Conspiracy: Personal and Social Transformation in the 1980's.* Jeremy P. Tarcher, Inc. Los Angeles, California, 1980.

Guralnik, David B., ed. in chief. *Webster's New World Dictionary of the American Language,* Second College Edition. Prentice Hall Press, Cleveland, Ohio. 1984.

Harman, Willis and Rheingold, Howard. *Higher Creativity: Liberating the Unconscious for Breakthrough Insights.* Jeremy P. Tarcher, Inc. Los Angeles, California. 1984.

Justice, Blair. "Those Who Stay Healthy." in *Noetic Sciences Review,* Summer, 1988. The Institute of Noetic Sciences. Sausalito, California.

Khanna, Suman. *Ghandi and the Good Life.* Ghandi Peace Foundation. New Delhi, India. 1985.

Kirsch, Jonathan. "Can Your Mind Cure Cancer?" in *New West,* January, 1977.

Krippner, Stanley. "'Set' Psychology and Human Potentials." in *Journal of Humanistic Psychology.* Fall 1986, Vol. 26, No. 4.

Krishnamurti, J. *Think on These Things.* Harper & Row, New York, 1964.

Pulos, Lee, "Visions of the Future Mind." Dreaming the New Dream Conference. San Francisco, California. Fall, 1988.

"Scientific Theories Suggest a Light at the End of the Tunnel." *The Tarrytown Letter,* March, 1982.

Siegal, Bernie S. *Love, Medicine & Miracles.* Harper & Row, Publishers. New York, New York, 1986. p. 3

Appendix of Exercises

ARE YOU CENTERED? QUIZ

1. Do you often feel sad or anxious for no apparent reason?
2. Do you sometimes feel like your life could spin out of control?
3. Do you ever feel like you might go crazy?
4. Are you plagued by worry?
5. Do you consistently feel people try to manipulate or put the screws to you?
6. Do you frequently feel stuck or taken for granted in your job or relationships?
7. Do you feel like you have to prove yourself all the time?
8. Do you often feel like you need to try harder?
9. Do you feel like your life is the same old unfulfilling thing day after day?
10. Do you often feel disconnected or anxious when you are with others?
11. Do you generally feel uncomfortable being alone?
12. Do you feel consumed with jealousy at times?
13. Do you often feel betrayed by others?
14. Do you often feel lonely even when you are with other people?
15. Do you often feel unfocused or without direction?
16. Do you frequently feel numb or dead inside?

From page 30.

CONSCIOUS CONNECTION EXERCISE

Sit back and close your eyes for a moment.

Take three deep breaths, and with each breath release any tension you are holding.

Imagine the sun above your head shining its warm golden light down upon you.

Allow every muscle in your body to relax as you feel this warm light washing over you.   *(pause)*

Imagine you have some magic dust.

Sprinkle it over yourself.

Imagine you have the power to feel any way you want.

You may have felt this way before. If so, recreate that feeling. If not, allow the dust to spontaneously create this feeling for you now.   *(pause)*

Choose a meaningful word or words that describe this feeling.

See yourself connected to your authentic self.   *(pause)*

Focus in on your image.
    See the details . . .
    Hear the sounds . . .
    Savor any smells or fragrances . . .
    Let yourself experience all the sensations that are part of
    your picture as you connect to your authentic self.

Take a long moment and let this experience saturate your being.
    (pause)

As you open your eyes, continue to consciously experience your image and feeling.

NOW . . . TAKE THREE DEEP BREATHS AND . . . . .

Close your eyes again. Imagine you have a movie camera.

Sharply focus in on your centering experience and all of its details.   *(pause)*

Run your movie in your mind now. This is what you will do whenever you want to be centered.

CONSCIOUS CONNECTION EXERCISE SUMMARIES

WORD(S)

FEELINGS

SOUNDS

SMELLS

OTHER SENSATIONS

COMPOSITE VISUAL IMAGE

CONSCIOUS CONNECTION: THREE STEP PROCESS

RELAX: Take three deep breaths and visualize the golden light washing over you.

RECALL: Your FEELINGS, SOUNDS, SMELLS, MEANINGFUL WORDS and VISUAL IMAGE

BE: Connected to your authentic self.

From pages 40, 41.

BELIEFS INVENTORY

WRITE IN YOUR NOTEBOOK ANY OF THE FOLLOWING STATEMENTS THAT ARE TRUE BASED ON YOUR IMMEDIATE RESPONSE. IF THERE IS ANY TRUTH TO THE STATEMENT, RECORD IT.

1. I sometimes think I am a bad person.
2. I am not lovable.
3. I do not deserve to be happy and fulfilled.
4. I am not important.
5. No matter what I do or how I do it, it is not enough.
6. Often, when I get what I want, I do not feel satisfied.
7. I will not allow myself to be happy and fulfilled if it makes someone close to me feel threatened.
8. When good things happen in my life, they never last.
9. I cannot overcome the negative effects of my heredity, past experiences, and relationships with people.
10. Someone or something often prevents me from getting what I want.
11. Others are able to get what they want, but not I.
12. I do not have enough time, money, talent or freedom to do what I want.
13. It is not possible for me to change.

In Questions 15-18, we are defining "struggle" not as a dynamic challenge, but as something frustrating, laborious and relentless.

14. Most of the time I experience life as painful.
15. Daily struggle makes me a better person.
16. Everything worthwhile requires a long struggle.
17. Life is a struggle.
18. If there were no struggle, I might get bored.

19. I will not do something unless I can do it perfectly.
20. If I do something that is less than perfect, I feel upset.

21. If I get close to someone, I might lose myself.
22. If I let myself get close to someone, they might leave me and I could not survive the hurt.

From pages 69-70.

SOURCE OF NEGATIVE BELIEF

1. When do I first remember thinking this way?

   Who was there? What was happening? What did I think was being said? (Message)

2. What did I decide about myself, others, or life as a result? (Belief/Decisions)

3. What did I feel? (Feeling)

From page 80.

WATCH YOUR BELIEFS IN ACTION

■ Practice observing your beliefs by watching, without criticism or judgement, how they operate in every aspect of your life. You will begin to see that all individual beliefs actually emanate from the five basic core beliefs.

■ Once you have isolated your beliefs by category, spend several days watching each belief manifest itself in your life. How does a belief affect your behavior? What are the ramifications of your actions?

■ Trace your core beliefs from their roots to the "branches" that govern your daily activities.

From page 92.

TRANSFORM YOUR NEGATIVE BELIEFS

■ IMPLANT POSITIVE BELIEFS IN YOUR MIND

■ ALLOW OLD, NEGATIVE BELIEFS TO EXIST SIMULTANEOUSLY

■ IMAGINE AND ACT ON NEW BELIEFS AS IF THEY WERE ALREADY TRUE, PRACTICING THEM IN TANDEM WITH YOUR CONSCIOUS CONNECTION

From page 97.

TRANSFORM YOUR NEGATIVE BELIEFS

1. Belief: I often think I am a bad person.

   (Core Belief: *I am not OK the way I am.*)

   Because I am OK the way I am, the bad things I've done are not about who I am.

2. Belief: I am not lovable.

   (Core Belief: *I am not OK the way I am.*)

   Because I am OK the way I am, I am lovable.

3. Belief: I do not deserve to be happy and fulfilled.

   (Core Belief: *I am not OK the way I am.*)

   Because I am OK the way I am, it is my birthright to be happy and fulfilled.

4. Belief: I am not important.

   (Core Belief: *I am not OK the way I am.*)

   Because I am OK the way I am, I am important.

5. Belief: No matter what I do or how I do it, it is not enough.

   (Core Belief: *I am not OK the way I am.*)

   Because I am OK the way I am, no proof is required.

6. Belief: Often, when I get what I want, I do not feel satisfied.

   (Core Belief: *I am not OK the way I am.*)

   Because I am OK the way I am, I love myself and feel fulfilled.

7. Belief: I will not allow myself to be happy and fulfilled if it makes someone close to me feel threatened.

   (Core Belief: *I am not OK the way I am.*)

   Because I am OK the way I am, I always have myself to count on.

8. Belief: When good things happen in my life, they never last.

   (Core Belief: *I am not in charge of my life.*)

   Because I am in charge of my life, I can continually make good things happen.

9. Belief: I cannot overcome the negative effects of my heredity, past experiences, and relationships with people.

   (Core Belief: *I am not in charge of my life.*)

   Because I am in charge of my life, I can determine how the past affects my present.

10. Belief: Often, someone or something prevents me from getting what I want.

    (Core Belief: *I am not in charge of my life.*)

    Because I am in charge of my life, I have the power to get what I want.

11. Belief: Others are able to get what they want, but not me.

    (Core Belief: *I am not in charge of my life.*)

    Because I am in charge of my life, I have as much chance of getting what I want as anyone else.

12. Belief: I do not have enough time, money, talent or freedom to do what I want.

    (Core Belief: *I am not in charge of my life.*)

    Because I am in charge of my life, I make the changes I choose.

13. Belief: It is not possible for me to change.

    (Core Belief: *I am not in charge of my life.*)

    Because I am in charge of my life, I make the changes I choose.

14. Belief: Most of the time I experience life as painful.

    (Core Belief: *Life is painful.*)

    Because I choose to see life as challenging and dynamic, I embrace its ebb and flow.

15. Belief: Daily struggle makes me a better person.

    (Core Belief: *Life is painful.*)

    Because I choose to see life as challenging and dynamic, I understand what I do is not who I am.

16. Belief: Everything worthwhile requires a struggle.

    (Core Belief: *Life is painful.*)

    Because I choose to see life as challenging and dynamic, I know only my best effort is required.

17. Belief: Life is difficult.

    (Core Belief: *Life is painful.*)

    Because I choose to see life as challenging and dynamic, it is.

18. Belief: If there were no struggle, I might get bored.

    (Core Belief: *Life is painful.*)

    Because I choose to see life as challenging and dynamic, I can create as much excitement as I choose.

19. Belief: I will not do something unless I can do it perfectly.

    (Core Belief: *I am not OK unless I am perfect.*)

    Because I know that what I do is not who I am, I can be satisfied and enjoy my best effort.

20. Belief: If I do something less than perfect, I feel upset.

    (Core Belief: *I am not OK unless I am perfect.*)

    Because I know that what I do is not who I am, I can relax and enjoy my best effort.

21. Belief: If I get close to someone, I might lose myself.

    (Core Belief: *It is too risky to be vulnerable.*)

    Because I have the power to take care of myself when I am vulnerable, I am safe.

22. Belief: If I let myself get close to someone, they might leave me and I could not survive the hurt.

(Core Belief: *It is too risky to be vulnerable.*)

Because I have the power to take care of myself when I am vulnerable, I know it is safe to take risks.

From pages 106-109.

INVOKING YOUR MUSE

Find a quiet place free of distractions, get consciously connected, and like Brahms, invoke the muse within you.

Notice how in the preparation phase, you can easily and clearly identify the problem to be solved.

In the incubation stage, observe how, when you are consciously connected, your penchant to continuously re-analyze is over—shadowed by your calm.

In the illumination stage, pay attention to how, when you are consciously connected, your "flashes" come through freely.

Maintain your connection through the verification stage.

From page 139.

TRUST QUESTIONNAIRE

IN YOUR NOTEBOOK, WRITE DOWN ANY STATEMENT THAT IS TRUE FOR YOU. BASE YOUR ANSWER ON WHAT IS TRUE MORE THAN 10% OF THE TIME.

---

1. I depend on recognition and approval from others to determine how I feel about myself.
2. I feel confused, unsure or worried about making decisions.
3. I allow others to make decisions for me.
4. I allow others to cancel out my decisions.
5. I consider my feelings unimportant.
6. My behavior is in conflict with my feelings.
7. I consider my thoughts unimportant.
8. My behavior is in conflict with my thoughts.
9. My feelings, thoughts, and behavior are in conflict with one another.

From pages 149-150.

AFFIRMATIVE STATEMENTS

---

1. I depend on my own recognition and approval to determine how I feel about myself.
2. I feel clear and calm when I make decisions.
3. I make my own decisions.
4. When I make a decision that is right for me, I adhere to it.
5. I consider my feelings important.
6. My behavior is in harmony with my feelings.
7. I consider my thoughts important.
8. My behavior is in harmony with my thoughts.
9. My feelings, thoughts, and behavior are in harmony.

From pages 150-151.

FORMULA FOR UNDERSTANDING VALUES

STEP ONE: IDENTIFICATION

The first task is to identify the values that guide your life now.

Divide a page in your notebook vertically into two sections. On the left side write the word VALUES on top, on the right hand side write the word ORIGIN. The following list of values gives some examples which may or may not apply to you. To get the most benefit from this exercise, take the time to add any values that are not on the list and any that you wish to strive towards in the future. Be sure to delete from the list any values that have no importance for you.

Examples

integrity	being loving
responsibility	health
forgiveness	beauty
intelligence	possessions
ambition	friendship
power	fun
excitement	privacy
independence	faith
sports	security
outwitting others	humor
notoriety	logic
courage	obedience
politeness	self-control
family	harmony

From page 158.

STEP TWO: ORIGIN

---

* Take each value from your list, one at a time, and think for a moment what would happen if you eliminated it. Would anyone disapprove, or be angry or disappointed with you? Would you be upset with yourself?

* In the right hand column of your worksheet, write who would feel strongly if you negated the value. It might be any or all of the following: another person, an institution, a culture or yourself. This is the origin of your present value.

* Think about what purpose the value serves or served for that person or institution.

* What was the context in which it originated for them?

From page 159.

STEP THREE: DISCRIMINATION

---

* Draw a line through those values you intend to completely eliminate.

* Organize your values into two groups by going through your list and putting number 1 by those values that are primary in your life right now. Mark the remaining values with a number 2.

* On the next page of your notebook, write LIFEVIEW at the top. Next divide the page in half horizontally and on the top half, write the words PRIMARY VALUES and on the bottom half, SECONDARY VALUES. Now, write your values in the appropriate sections.

* Over time, the priority you place on specific values may change. Mark values that you would like to see become less important with zeros and those you want to become more important with stars.

From pages 161-162.

STEP FOUR: ACTION

---

* DECIDING WHICH VALUE OR VALUES ARE RELEVANT: When a situation arises in which you feel uncomfortable, confused or challenged, and do not immediately know what to do, begin by identifying the value or values that are meaningful in that particular instance. Establish whether they are of primary or secondary importance.

* POSTULATING RESULTS: Speculate on the outcome of acting on each value by playing the situation through in your imagination and observing what effect each value has upon it. Consider the other people involved and, most important, your feelings about yourself.

* CHOOSING A SUITABLE VALUE OR VALUES: After examining the hypothetical result connected with each relevant value, select the one (or more) values that is most in harmony with your thoughts and feelings. You will instinctively know which value (or values) is right for you. Remember that intuition is a form of inner knowledge. Trust and pay attention to your inner self.

From pages 163-164.

APPLYING VALUES TO DAILY LIFE

---

* What values are triggered as you think about how to respond?

* What would be the outcome of the actions associated with each value?

* Does one value take precedence over the other in this circumstance?

* How would you respond?

From page 168.

THORN IN YOUR SIDE

Pick a situation that is currently a thorn in your side, one that is uncomfortable and unsettling. Take a deep breath and bring your connection into your being by repeating the word, sensations and image you chose. Repeat them over and over again. Pay no attention to anything else. Now play the thorny situation through in your mind, using your connection as a backdrop for that old, familiar scene. Within the new context of your connection, how will you behave? What outcome do you predict?

From page 177.

Index

About the Authors

Dr. Lotery graduated from Ohio State University with a Bachelor of Arts in Psychology and attained her Masters in Social Work from Arizona State University. She was awarded her Doctorate in Clinical Psychology from the Cambridge Graduate School of Psychology, Los Angeles. Beginning in Phoenix and now in Los Angeles and Santa Barbara, she has been in private practice since 1977 working with individuals, couples and groups. She has worked as a therapist in psychiatric hospitals, both public and private. With an extensive background in psychotherapy and crisis counseling, Fran has taught both at the undergraduate as well as graduate level, and supervised psychological interns. Presently, she lives with her husband Rex and their son in Santa Barbara, California. Fran has two step-children and four grandchildren.

Dr. Melchiorre received her Bachelor of Science Degree from Western Reserve University, Cleveland, Ohio, and a Bachelor of Arts in Psychology from Pepperdine University in Los Angeles. She earned a Masters Degree in Marriage, Family and Child Counseling at Azusa Pacific College, Los Angeles, and was awarded her doctorate in Clinical

Psychology from the California Graduate Institute in Los Angeles. Dr Melchiorre is a certified clinical member of the International Transactional Analysis Association and has trained all over the country with such recognized medical and psychological experts as Robert and Mary Goulding, Irving and Miriam Poster, and Muriel James. Working with individuals, couples and groups, Sherry has been in private practice for over twenty years. She and her husband Michael now divide their time between Los Angeles and Santa Barbara. She has three grown children and three grandchildren.

ORDERING INFORMATION

LIVE INSIDE OUT ■ *NOT UPSIDE DOWN* is so important you may want to order copies for those you know are interested in change. Order through your local bookstore or BookWorld Services, Inc., 1933 Whitfield Park Avenue., Sarasota, FL 34243:

🖳 Fax orders: 800-777-2525

☎ Tel. orders: 800-444-2524

Qty.

_____ @$24.95 = _____ *Live Inside Out* ■ *Not Upside Down*

_____ @ $9.95 = _____ Audio Cassette: Conscious Connection Exercise & Problem solving exercises

_____ @ $9.95 = _____ *Live Inside Out* ■ *Not Upside Down Workbook*

_____ @$15.00 = _____ SET: Audio cassette and Workbook

_____ Sales Tax (Florida residents only)

_____ Shipping and Handling: $3.95 for first item, $2.00 each additional item, $6.00 for set of book, tape and workbook.*

_____ TOTAL

*Allow 7–10 working days for book post. UPS is $4.95 per book, allow 4–5 working days

Payment

☐ Cheque

☐ Credit Card: ☐ VISA ☐ MasterCard ☐ Discover
☐ Diners ☐ Optima

Card Number: _____ Exp. Date _____

Name on Card: _____

Dr. Lotery and Dr. Melchiorre are available for consulting, seminars, lectures and media through Bronze Publishing, 1187 Coast Village Rd., Suite 1422C, Santa Barbara, California, 93108, Tel.: 310-476-0955.

The authors welcome feedback and questions from readers.

Prices subject to change.